ZACARIAS, MY BROTHER

ZACARIAS, MY BROTHER

the making of a terrorist

Abd Samad Moussaoui
with Florence Bouquillat

Translated by
Simon Pleasance & Fronza Woods

Seven Stories Press
New York

Copyright © 2003 by Abd Samad Moussaoui and Florence Bouquillat

A Seven Stories Press First Edition

All rights reserved. No part of this book may be reproduced, stored in a retrieval system, or transmitted in any form, by any means, including mechanical, electric, photocopying, recording or otherwise, without the prior written permission of the publisher.

Seven Stories Press
140 Watts Street
New York, NY 10013
www.sevenstories.com

In Canada:
Hushion House, 36 Northline Road, Toronto, Ontario M4B 3E2

Library of Congress Cataloging-in-Publication Data

Moussaoui, Abd Samad, 1967–
[Zacarias Moussaoui, mon frère. English]
Zacarias, my brother: the making of a terrorist / Abd Samad Moussaoui; with Florence Bouquillat; translated by Simon Pleasance and Fronza Woods.—1st ed.
    p.   cm.
ISBN: 1-58322-585-4 (pbk.)
1. Moussaoui, Zacarias, 1968–   2. Terrorists—France—Biography. 3. Terrorism—United States. 4. Terrorism—Religious aspects—Islam. I. Bouquillat. II. Title.
HV6433.F7M6813 2003
973.931'092—dc21   2003009144

9 8 7 6 5 4 3 2 1

College professors may order examination copies of Seven Stories Press titles for a free six-month trial period. To order, visit www.sevenstories.com/textbook, or fax on school letterhead to (212) 226-1411.

Printed in Canada.

CONTENTS

PUBLISHER'S NOTE

Zacarias Moussaoui is Abd Samad Moussaoui's brother.

Zacarias Moussaoui is currently being held in a United States prison on six charges stemming from the attacks of September 11, 2001. Four of these charges are capital offenses, punishable by death. As of this writing, Moussaoui is the only person to be charged in connection with those attacks.

In a letter to his mother from prison, Zacarias wrote, "As far as the American story is concerned, I haven't done anything wrong and I shall prove as much when the time comes *insha'Allah*.... I am patiently awaiting the moment to prove my innocence."[*]

He is accused of preparing acts of terrorism; conspiring with intent to hijack an aircraft; destroying an aircraft; using weapons of mass destruction; murdering United States officials; and destroying property. A federal prosecutor is duly making moves to demand the death penalty.

The presumption is that Moussaoui was the famous "20th hijacker," the one who was to have been on board the September 11 suicide airplane that crashed in a field in Pennsylvania.

On that day, Moussaoui was behind bars in a Shelburne County jail in Minnesota, where he had been held for twenty-five days.

---

[*] Frédéric Chambon, "Entre New York et Narbonne, l'échange épistolaire entre Aïcha et Zacarias Moussaoui," *Le Monde,* 18 November 2001. ["Between New York and Narbonne, correspondence of Aïcha and Zacarias Moussaoui."]

Up until his arrest on August 16, 2001, Moussaoui had been attending piloting courses at the Pan Am International Flight Academy, near Minneapolis. One of his instructors, a former Air Force officer, found his behavior suspicious and alerted the police.

Technically, Moussaoui was arrested for "irregular status and working illegally." So he was first charged and detained for breach of immigration laws.

He had arrived to the United States at a Chicago airport on February 23, 2001, with a French passport. Moussaoui was authorized to remain in the U.S. for 90 days, until May 22, 2001. His passport bore a visa apparently issued by the United States embassy in Pakistan.

On August 21, 2001, shortly after his arrest, the FBI contacted the French secret police. They learned that Moussaoui traveled to Afghanistan in 1999, and to Pakistan. FBI agents had determined, during the summer of 2001, that the United States was in danger of an imminent attack by Islamic extremists. They considered the risk that airplanes would be hijacked. One FBI report even referred to the possibility that Zacarias Moussaoui might "fly something into the World Trade Center."[*]

Abd Samad Moussaoui, who has no time for extremist ideologies—indeed, he campaigns against them—has lost all contact with his brother, whom he last saw in 1995. With Zacarias Moussaoui's trial fast approaching, his brother has attempted to shed some light on the reasons why a life can change so radically and to warn against the destructive ideologies threatening the international community.

---

[*] Eric Leser, "La police fédérale en accusation," *Le Monde,* 16-17 June 2002.

PREFACE

September 13, 2001. A Thursday. I'd finished my week's classes and tidied up the little room I use at the high school. For the past few days I'd been working as an assistant teacher, teaching electrical engineering at the vocational school in Mende, about sixty miles north of Montpellier, where I live with my wife. I was driving home.

Night was falling over the Millau plateau. As always when the weather's clear over these highlands, the sky was thick with twinkling stars. I had the radio on because, like everyone else, I needed to know how the world was faring since the atrocious attacks on the World Trade Center and the Pentagon. On the Larzac plateau the journalist's voice faded—thereabouts the airwaves can get lost in the vastness.

I made the most of the silence, letting my mind wander. Then all of a sudden, coming from who knows where, a voice intruded on my pleasant musings. That voice was talking about me. It uttered my name, "Moussaoui."

Actually, it was my brother's name that the voice was broadcasting for all to hear: "Zacarias Moussaoui." Unbelievable! My own brother! Was I dreaming? No, it was a nightmare. The start of a nightmare.

"Zacarias Moussaoui, a French citizen of Algerian origin, was arrested in the United States on August 16th. He is allegedly linked with the attacks on the Pentagon and the World Trade Center…"

I couldn't think straight. My brain was a muddle. I drove, concentrating on the road ahead. My hands gripped the steering wheel. There was a faint hope: my Zacarias Moussaoui, my brother, is not of Algerian origin. We're French, but of Moroccan origin. The Moussaoui they were talking about had to be someone with the same name. That had to be it. It couldn't be him.

But deep inside I was worried. Unfortunately I knew that it wasn't impossible; I knew it might be my Zacarias.

"Hailing from Narbonne, in southern France, Zacarias Moussauoi was arrested while he was attending flying school."

Hailing from Narbonne. Could it be that someone with the same name as my brother *also* came from that city? I didn't want to think about it. I just wanted to get home, and be with my wife and our friends.

That was a year ago. And for the past year the media have been hounding me with endless questions. Here in France and around the world, they have been talking about Zacarias Moussaoui, my brother. They've also been talking about me, Abd Samad. My heart feels like there's a weight on it. Something hard to describe; something powerful that I can no longer suppress.

Little by little in my solitude, without thinking about it too much, I've moved toward the only possible way of getting this burden off my chest. I've decided to write. So here I am, a simple person, wanting to share what I know about my brother, addressing you, my readers. Who is my brother? What's his story? How could he ever get mixed up in all that horror? Could it have been avoided? I want to try and sketch some answers to all these questions. So I'll tell you something about our life. I'll tell you what my grandmother, my mother's mother, my aunt and my uncles have all been saying out loud about our family history. I hope I will be able to make myself understood.

1

A FAMILY

My maternal grandmother's name is Amina. In Arabic, *amina* means serene, peaceful. The name suits her well. My grandmother is a character, in the fullest sense of the word. She comes from a noble lineage—if you trace her genealogy from one generation to the next, you end up at Moulay Idriss, the great saint descended from Prophet Muhammad [ﷺ].* The descendants of the prophet are the Cherif, the family of the kings of Morocco.

Amina was born in Tafilelt, in Morocco's far south, ninety years ago. Needless to say, Amina lived through the colonial period. She readily tells how, in the 1920s, Tafilelt stood up to French colonization. She recalls the Foreign Legion's bombardments and the battles between French and Moroccan troops. Early in the colonial period, the region was struck by famine. So Amina's family moved, heading off to the Middle Atlas and settling in Azrou, a rugged village high in the mountains. In winter, the alleys of Azrou are filled with snow. It was in Azrou that Amina met my grandfather. He was her second husband. My grandmother doesn't talk much about her first one, with whom she had one daughter, Rouqayyah. My grandfather was

---

* The symbol of *salla-llâhou ^alayhi wasallam.* This is an invocation of Prophet Muhammad meaning: "May God honor him and raise him ever higher and may He preserve his community from what He fears for it."

called Mekki, "the man from Mecca." He was a lot older than my grandmother, maybe twenty years her senior. He was a widower. In those days widows and widowers didn't stay widows and widowers for long.

Mekki came from a well-off family, and owned several butcher shops in the region. He wasn't afraid of hard work. And he was a good man, renowned for his great generosity to the poor. Those in need would travel many miles, on donkey or by foot, in sun and snow, across the mountains to ask him for help. Mekki would give them meat to feed their children. He was a practicing Muslim for whom it was a spiritual requirement to give help to the poorest.

Mekki also liked working his land. And it was on his land that death claimed him in 1953, in the middle of harvest. My grandmother was just forty, with five children—her daughter from the first marriage and four children by my grandfather; Muhammad, the eldest of the boys; then Omar; my mother Aïcha; and my aunt Zouhour. My mother was saddled with the task of bringing up all five of them. Alone—and to everybody's surprise poor, because Mekki had not managed to put one *sou* aside. The first thing Amina did was to sell the remaining butcher shop. Then, being good with her hands, she started making *canouns*, terra cotta braziers which all cooks used then. She sold them at market, gradually earning a livelihood. But she was poor.

My mother was about seven, and my aunt four, when my grandfather died. My two uncles were a bit older. I say "about," because birth registers in those days were not as accurate as they are today. Because my grandmother was unable to feed everybody with her meager income, a cousin offered to take my mother into his home and raise her. Needless to say, by way of exchange, Aïcha had to help with the housework.

So my mother grew up separated from her parents. At a very young age she began looking for something better. Aïcha had just turned fourteen when she met my father, Omar Moussaoui. He was from Fès, some forty miles from Azrou. Fès is a large city, renowned throughout Morocco and abroad for its tiles and mosaics, and above all for the Qarawiyyin theological university. My father was a tiler, who traveled a great deal in the region for his work. That's how he met my mother.

Aïcha wanted to get married right away. At first, my grandmother refused. Aïcha was fourteen, and to my grandmother she was still a little girl. But in those days, in a southern Moroccan village, marrying off daughters that young was not uncommon. Aïcha dug her heels in, and my grandmother finally agreed to the marriage—that, anyway, is the story as told by my grandmother and my uncles and aunts. It's not at all my mother's version. Throughout our childhood, Aïcha told my siblings and me that she had been "forced" to marry at the age of fourteen.

Soon after she was married, my mother gave birth to two children, who died very young. Then, when she was about seventeen, she had Nadia, my eldest sister. Two years later my other sister, Jamila, was born. It was then that my father heard about the possibility of work in France. The year was 1965 and French recruiters were going from village to village, explaining to people that France was looking for craftsmen, masons and tilers. They said that France was a rich country where the pay was good. In Morocco, my father made a good living. He even had a motorbike! But he thought that working in France would bring in more money, so he and my mother decided to move. Once again, I know all these details through my grandmother, my aunt and my uncles. My mother told us no more than that she had learned to sew, that she had been forced into marriage, that our father was a hard man, that her mother was mean and that she had been brought up by a cousin.

The Moussaoui family settled in Bayonne and my father found

work straightaway with a tiling and building company. He was very good at his job. He could pour an eighty-foot-square concrete screed, and could pick out the tiniest flaw or lump by sight, without even using a level. In no time he was making good money and he managed to buy himself a Renault. I remember the car well because of the time we wrecked it. The car rolled and landed on its roof, and we all crawled out through the back window. I also have clear memories of the huge color TV set which had the place of honor in the living room.

I was born two years after my parents and my sisters arrived in France, on the first of January, 1967, at half past midnight. I am told that the doctor came to our house in his party clothes. My brother Zacarias was born in St. Jean de Luz on May 30, 1968. Three years later my parents were divorced. I have no memories of domestic violence, but I was very young at the time. What I do remember is the day my mother told us, "We're going to a resort." "We" meant she and her children. So all five of us left home and went to the Dordogne. I was four and Zacarias three. Aïcha had found a job as a laundress at the resort, and small lodgings. I don't remember her ever explaining to us that she had left my father; we simply weren't living with him any more.

It was summer, and there were bikes in the camp for us to ride. It was like a holiday, a totally different atmosphere because my father wasn't there. I don't have many memories of him; Zacarias can't have any at all, because he was so young when we left. When September came we went even further away, to Mulhouse in Alsace, because my mother had found a job there. I don't know how and I don't know what the job was.

No sooner had we arrived in Alsace than my mother put my two sisters, my brother and me in an orphanage, run by the local Social Services Department. She couldn't afford keep us with her. So from one day to the next, we found ourselves both fatherless and motherless. The few memories I have of those grim childhood years are dreadful ones. We had the feeling that we were not like the other kids. Zacarias and I looked at them as if they were Martians! And even the youth workers seemed strange to us. I remember that first year they came and woke us up at midnight, to celebrate my fifth birthday. They had made mulled wine. I have assorted other memories, of the way the rooms were furnished, of the wooden floors and the spiral staircases. We slept two to a room. The boys' building was separated from the girls' by a courtyard, overlooked by the cafeteria. I spent all my time with my brother—Thank God they didn't separate us! Zacarias was quite small. My sisters lived in the girls' building, but we would meet up during the day. My big sister Nadia watched over us as best as she could. Perhaps my mother had told her to keep an eye on us.

It has to be said that all sorts of things went on in that orphanage. Some of the older children took drugs, and others prostituted themselves. We took great care not to be like them, not to use the vulgar language they did, and to avoid the mean ones. Many of the children were suffering from a lack of emotional warmth.

Zac and I were always together, be it in the yard or the cafeteria. We played a lot of ball games—bench-ball and soccer. We also had stilts. Our best game was stilt fights. He and I lived through that year as if in a dream. We didn't really understand what we were doing in the orphanage. But we had a pretty good hunch that our situation wasn't altogether normal. With every passing day we would say over and over that we weren't going to stay long, we were quite sure about that, our mother had promised us. Every day we would nag Nadia to find out when our mother was going to come and fetch us, and she would patiently answer, "Soon." But we were a bit worried from time to time. I don't recall my mother taking us home for weekends. She came to see us about once a week, but she never took us back home. Maybe she did not yet have a place of her own.

One day, after about a year, she really did come for us. Oddly enough, I recall no details of the departure. I do remember that we moved to the Rue des Châtaigniers, into a rather classy building. There were nice carpets and there was a lift with big mirrors. We had a large apartment on the fourth floor. The contrast was striking. For Zacarias and me, our mother was a heroine, a fighter who did everything she could for her children and made sacrifices for our happiness.

Aïcha found a job as a cleaning woman in the central post office in Mulhouse. The inspector in her department was a man named Joseph Klifa. Later he would become mayor and win fame for opposing the extreme right in the region, as part of the republican alliance. Klifa felt sorry for my mother. She was a woman on her own with four children, and would tell anyone who would listen that she had been forced into marriage in Morocco. One fine day, after she had obtained French nationality, Klifa helped her to get a permanent position. She became a post office employee.

She had a second job at night after the post office closed. So my sister Nadia, now twelve, took over my mother's role at home. She did the shopping and the cooking and cleaning, and looked after us. At night she made us supper and in the morning she helped us get dressed. And there was no messing about or else the slaps fell thick and fast! My other sister, Jamila, backed her up. It took both of them to keep an eye on Zacarias and me.

We soon moved house again, this time to an apartment in the Bourtzwiller project. Bourtzwiller was what is now called "a problem neighborhood." At the time, Zacarias and I thought only about having fun. We went to school to have fun, and we came out of school and had more fun. Boys will be boys.

At our school there was a notorious family with seventeen children by the name of Deau. It was better not to cross them, because if you got in an argument with one, the other sixteen would come to his aid. Zacarias did get into a fight with the Deau boy his age, and in no time things escalated: the Deau boy called his big brother, and Zacarias called me. Then the second Deau called his even bigger brother, so I had to call for help from my sister Jamila. She was awesome when it came to defending us. She could pack a punch as well as any boy. And if that didn't do the trick, we could call Nadia. Unfortunately, Nadia was our last trump card, and they still had at least thirteen.

At school, we pulled a lot of stunts. One September, all the kids in the neighborhood agreed that term was starting too early. So we put our heads together, and came up with a plan. A day or two before we were due back, some of the kids broke into the school. They put all the chairs and tables in one classroom, and painstakingly spraypainted them. And it worked! The beginning of term was delayed for a week.

Zac and I liked to have bike races, but because our bikes were too big (they were salvaged) we had to lean left and then right to reach the pedals. It really hurt was when you missed a pedal! We were reckless. Our favorite game was to climb along the drain pipes up to the roof as quickly as we could. We raced the other boys to prove our bravery and agility.

Many of the families in our housing project came from North Africa. We got along well, except for the families renowned for their dislike of foreigners. In our building there was the Kol family; the parents were very racist. And when Alsatians are racist, it's quite something! Whenever the Kols bumped into Zac and me they called us "dirty niggers." Not "dirty Arabs," but "dirty niggers." They didn't make any distinction between Arabs and Blacks, we were simply

Not White. One day, for no particular reason, the eldest Kol son, who must have been fifteen or sixteen, insulted us, setting off a general brawl. He was really mean and quite a lot bigger than us. In the free-for-all, he threw me against an iron post which got stuck in my back. I ended up in the hospital, and I've still got the scar.

Near the Bourtzwiller projects there were some ponds. We built rafts and had sea battles. For us real life happened outdoors. In the apartment was not much; my mother didn't have a lot of time for us. She always had other things to do. It would have been misguided to expect the slightest tender word from her, or the merest gesture of affection. She didn't know how to do that. She often scolded my sisters, who did so much work. So Zac and I kept to ourselves, giving each other support and sometimes giving our elder sister a little bit of thanks. At school we did nothing, or next to nothing. It wasn't until my fifth year of primary school, when I was ten or eleven, that I realized that it was better to work a little. Zacarias realized it too.

Our father came to see us now and then. Or rather, he *tried* to see us in Bourtzwiller. For us it was a kind of a game, with strict rules laid down by my mother. She had trained us. She told us that our father had hurt her, that he was a hard man and that she would be greatly upset if we agreed to see him. So when my father came, we would run off, just as she had told us to. All four of us, all in different directions. We were running away from the big bad wolf. Poor man!

I remember one episode particularly well. My father had given us advance notice that he was coming, that he had visiting rights. My mother told us, "Okay, he'll here about two P.M., so just before that, you all disappear." We obeyed her. When my father arrived and realized that we weren't in the apartment, instead of wasting time arguing with my mother he started looking for us everywhere in the neighborhood. He had travelled miles to see us. (Maybe he didn't even know that we were hiding. Maybe he thought that my mother hadn't told us he was coming.) When he finally found us, he said, "Come on, let's have a walk together!" And we ran away again, just like that. But this time he ran after us, caught us, and put us into his car. He started the motor, and Zac and I exchanged a single glance, there being no need for words in so perilous a situation. At the same instant, we opened the car doors and leapt out. If we hadn't done that, we would no longer have been our mother's sons!

Scenes like this were repeated many times. Until my father finally gave up, I think. Until he understood that my mother had turned us against him. He must have told himself that when we were old enough, we would decide for ourselves if we wanted to see him. From that moment on our mother changed her tune, telling us constantly, "Well! See how your father's abandoned you!"

About that time, my mother met another man, Saïd, who moved in with us. My mother worked, received welfare allowances, and was extremely thrifty. She eventually managed to buy a small house, a freestanding home of the kind built for workers in the old potash mines, in the very heart of Mulhouse. I can even remember the price, 120,000 francs—it was all my mother talked about. The house had two upper stories and a large garden with a shed we fixed up. It was at 8 Rue du Kaysersberg, near the Boulevard Stoessel.

Saïd was like a father to us. At least he was the guy who stayed longest. He was nice enough and he didn't bother us. Come what may, it was my mother who wore the pants. It was *her* very own house, as she never failed to remind him. He worked at Peugeot and when he wasn't at the factory, he tended his rented vegetable plot. We went there every weekend. It was his great love, working his private patch of land. He was originally from the Rif Mountains, a farming region in northern Morocco. I think my mother and he must have sold some of the produce, because we didn't eat much of it. Our daily fare tended to be buttered bread and coffee with milk. My mother never stopped saying how she had to keep putting money away.

One day, Saïd wanted to take me to work with him on the plot. I didn't feel like going, but he forced me to sit on his lap in the car. Somehow he managed to drive with me wriggling around on his knees, but once we got to the end of the street, I bit him—causing him to lose control and drive the car straight into a tree. The Peugeot was totalled.

Near the projects were slag heaps which locals called Mont Coqrourie. They were large mounds with trees and a little stream. We heard tales about the place which alarmed and intrigued us. So our great challenge was to go in there; you had to show how brave you were by crossing the Coqrourie. Once inside, the slightest noise would make us run off as fast as our legs could carry us, shouting, "They're there! They're there!" And all the neighborhood kids would scram, like rabbits.

We had rollerskates and skateboards. We also "collected" racing bikes, always too big for us, which we took wherever we found them. We would throw them into the canal, right close to the edge. Then we would go home, and in the evening we would ask our stepfather to walk with us beside the canal. My brother and I would exclaim, "Oh! A bike in the canal!" Our stepfather would help us drag it from the water, happy at our godsend. So we had at least a dozen bikes at home. Every time we went off for a walk, we would "find" a bike. Of course my stepfather caught on, and one day, after dragging a bicycle out of the water for Zacarias, Saïd said, "But that's my bike, I'm the one who got it out!" Zacarias was dumbfounded.

Another time, on my way home from school, I didn't feel like walking and I spied a small bike. Without a moment's hesitation, I took it, rode it home, and chucked it into the canal as usual. But this time somebody had seen me. The owner turned up at our house and found Nadia and Zacarias. He said to them, "Someone saw your brother take the bike. He'd better give it back right away." When I got home my brother asked me about it, and I told him it wasn't true. He believed me. He was furious. He went to see the owner of the bike, and cried, "How can you accuse my brother of being a thief! He didn't do it. If he did, I'd know about it! You can't accuse someone without any proof, that's a false accusation, and it's serious for my brother's reputation in the neighborhood." Incredible reasoning coming from an eight-year-old. To think, my little brother, lecturing a grown-up to get me off the hook! And it was because that injustice shocked him. Suddenly the guy started to have doubts, and he dropped the whole thing. Later, when I told Zacarias the truth, he bawled me out.

But the favorite sport of the neighborhood kids was to attack vans with sling shots. One day, a driver turned his vehicle right around and gave chase. He caught up with us, leapt out of the van like a madman and grabbed me by the neck. I was scared stiff, but because I'd already got rid of the sling shot, I yelled, "It wasn't me! It wasn't me!" Once again, my brother came to my rescue, telling the driver, "It wasn't him, it's a serious matter to accuse people without proof!" But this time around the guy wasn't having any of it. He took my brother and me home, where my mother reprimanded us in front of him. And then, as soon as his back was turned, she hissed, "We don't give a damn about that guy. Get out of here!"

My sister Nadia attended secondary school when we lived at Bourtzwiller. The headmaster said that she was his best student. She was tall and had black, frizzy hair. A pretty girl, she danced and acted. Later on, in Mulhouse, we all went to see her perform in her first play.

Jamila was something different, though; things were not as easy for her. When my brother and I were small, there was an alliance between our sisters: the two big kids against the two little ones. And then one day all that changed. My sisters turned on each other, and my mother turned on Jamila. Who got scolded when one of us did something silly? Jamila. Who got slapped? Jamila. Zacarias and I felt sorry for her.

It was when we went to live on Rue du Kaysersberg that the situation between Jamila and my mother became really poisoned. It all started over a croissant. Every morning my mother bought a croissant at the bakery on her way to work. The croissant cost two francs, and every night she put a two-franc coin in her wallet. But one morning, the coin wasn't there. She didn't bother to find out who had taken it, and immediately laid into Jamila (who wasn't the culprit). My mother was furious.

Divide and rule was my mother's strategy. But it didn't work at all with Zacarias and me. We were so close to one another that she got nowhere when she tried to favor one over the other. She found it easier to divide her daughters. She had a real technique. She would take one of them aside and say, "You are the most beautiful. You are my favorite." Then she would do the same thing with the other. To punish us, my mother would often use a strap.

Zacarias was an ideal younger brother. He was smart, clever and kind. I think that we just knew, without ever saying as much out loud, that in this life we could only really count on each other. We tried to avoid getting mixed up in family feuds. We knew them to be a source of pain, screams, and blows. We were often quite naughty, but never in a mean or violent way. We just did the naughty things kids do, to have a laugh, not to do any harm.

In 1974 we returned to Morocco, our country of origin, for our first summer trip. I have wonderful memories of the journey there.

We set off by train, all five of us. I was seven and Zacarias five-and-a-half. It was very hot and there were water vendors in the Spanish stations. Again, Nadia organized everything down to the last detail.

Once in Morocco, I remember my aunt's cakes, huge watermelons, and prickly pear fruit. The weather was very fine and we played in the streets with our cousins. Pure bliss, an outstanding summer.

In Morocco, the sort of things my mother said changed completely. She who usually grumbled about working herself to death and how hard life was would tell the whole family that we had a very comfortable life in France; that money grew on trees there; and that all you needed to succeed was desire.

Throughout our stays there, our grandmother and our aunt attended our every need. They didn't get to see us often and as soon as we arrived they would start spoiling us, Zacarias especially, because he was the youngest. They gave us homemade pastries, *makrouds*, honey and almond cakes, and *zlabias*—colorful, translucent sweets made of pure sugar. Sometimes when my mother wasn't looking, they would give us a little pocket money and we would slip away and buy sweets at the corner shop.

On Sundays we went with our cousins to the Koranic school, though Zacarias and I hardly knew what the Koran was. We liked it, and found it very unusual at the same time: all those children in a large room, repeating after the teacher the verses of that mysterious, holy book. There were children of all ages there, the smallest at the front, the biggest at the back. The master used reeds of different lengths to reach each head. That's where we first heard the chant, "*Bismillah ar-Rahman ar-Rahim,*" (In the name of God the compassionate, the merciful), which we memorized quickly and repeated with great vigor. Those were lovely times.

I remember heading to Morocco one summer in the car with my stepfather, when I was about ten. It's a long way from Mulhouse to

Taourirt. Zacarias and I slipped into the back of the station wagon to get some sleep among the luggage.

Back in France, Zacarias and I began to badger our mother to sign us up for sports. First we did judo and karate; then Zacarias played handball and I played basketball.

For Zacarias, handball quickly became more than a sport—it was his passion. He was brilliant. He played guard, a difficult position. One of his old handball pals, Thomas, who subsequently played in the first division, remembers Zacarias very well, particularly because he had a particular mannerism: when he played he would stick out the tip of his tongue, and bite it as he hit the ball. Everybody was afraid that a bad shot would cut his tongue off! Zacarias's gifts were unanimously recognized by his trainers, his teammates, and especially his opponents. Zacarias competed in various tournaments and his team won first the district championships, then the Alsace championships. I loved going to watch him play, to support him. For Zacarias, the future was all mapped out. He would study and play sports.

Things got worse and worse between our mother and Jamila. As soon as they bumped into each other in the house, they started quarrelling. Aïcha had taken a sudden dislike to her daughter. Jamila started to run away from home, and every time it was up to Zacarias and me to find her. One Sunday, my mother came into my bedroom to talk, the way she did whenever she wanted me to help her sort out a problem. "Okay, I'd like you to do me a favor. I'm going to send your sister away to school, because this just isn't working. She's rude and ill-mannered, and she doesn't study a bit. I can't cope with her anymore. Boarding school will be good for her. Do you want to go too, so that she won't be all alone?" It seemed a good idea to me for Jamila to go. It could only make things better between them.

My choice was quickly made. There was no question of my mother being separated from Nadia, whom she loved and who was useful. And Zacarias was too young to be a boarder. Since I didn't have the heart to let my sister go off alone, I agreed to my mother's proposal. Zacarias was sad when I left, because it was a bit like I was abandoning him. But neither did he want his favorite sister to end up alone at a boarding school. He was forced to admit that there really wasn't any other choice.

So the following term my sister and I went to school in Altkirch, a little village twelve miles from Mulhouse. We boarded during the week, coming home on weekends. I started in the sixth grade, Jamila in fourth grade. The beginning was hard—I missed Zacarias and he missed me. He was bored without his brother and found it harder to elude the domestic turmoil. He was on his own. Luckily for him, he had handball.

For Jamila and me it wasn't all unpleasant, though. It was something of an adventure, our apprenticeship in freedom. That was the year I smoked my first cigarette.

Zacarias and I hugged every time we were reunited. We made sure that we spent all weekend with each other. I especially made a point to attend his handball matches.

Zacarias rarely told me the details of his rows with my mother; probably he was ashamed. He did admit that without me there, it was difficult to dodge her fits of anger. No matter how hard he tried, he didn't always manage to.

Toward the end of the year, my mother gathered us all together one weekend to tell us that she wanted to apply at the post office for a job transfer. She said she wanted to go somewhere sunny. Only Zacarias spoke up: "I won't go. Next year I want to study sports at Mulhouse." My mother ignored him. She took out a map of France to show us several cities she could apply to be transferred to:

Montpellier, Narbonne, Perpignan, and Béziers. We used a ruler to check which city was closest to the sea; Narbonne was the winner. My mother called for a vote. Zacarias was the only one against moving. Together with my sisters, I imagined the sea and sun, a year-round holiday. We didn't care a bit about leaving Mulhouse. Zacarias was the only one who was attached to that city. In hindsight, after the orphanage, that move to Narbonne was wrenching for him. It meant the end of his dream of becoming a professional handball player, and perhaps a coach.

2

TEENAGE YEARS: FUN TIMES AND FRUSTRATIONS

We moved in late August. I was thirteen, and Zacarias was twelve. For weeks before we finally left Mulhouse, as we were packing up, he grumbled, "I don't want to go there. Narbonne's a dump. Anyway, I'm not going! I want to stay in Mulhouse." Needless to say, he had to come with us. From that moment on, something in Zacarias changed. There was a sort of uncertainty about him, an edge of bitterness and rancor. Like a very fine scar, hardly visible, which never heals. Zacarias missed life in Mulhouse—or rather, the life he had imagined.

When we left Mulhouse our living conditions changed overnight. In Alsace, we had a large house with a big garden and a shed. We all had our own rooms. In Narbonne we rediscovered "the charms of the projects," the real, sordid thing, just like in TV reports. The first time we walked into our apartment in the Razimbaud projects we were a bit shocked to open the bathroom door and see, front and center, a sitz bath.* We'd never seen anything quite so ridiculous!

We now had to share rooms, Zac and me in one, Nadia and Jamila in the other. We were happy at first just to look around in the

---

* A *baignoire sabot,* or sitz bath, is a low, small bathtub with a ledge, once common in France.

few weeks before school started. When our mother had time, she took us to the sea. Then we started at the nearby Montesquieu secondary school. It was difficult to start all over as complete strangers again. Zacarias was enrolling in the sixth grade and was even more nervous than I. Our Alsatian accent was a major disadvantage. It was impossible to go unnoticed with an accent like that. What's more, we were the only "Blacks" in Narbonne who spoke with the accent; the contrast, needless to say, made everybody laugh—except us. Shopkeepers, certain teachers, our neighbors, but above all our classmates considered us oddities.

I use the term "Blacks," even though we are Arabs, because that's the way most born-and-bred French people saw us. It was hard to label us at a glance. The only thing that was clear was that we come from somewhere else. From Africa, or from the Caribbean? I've lived with this ambiguity my whole life, and so has Zacarias. Now that I'm an adult and settled, it no longer bothers me—I've got used to it. But as children, Zacarias and I found it extremely unpleasant to be forced so often to explain our origins. There was something humiliating and unsettling about it—it was as if we didn't have any formal identity. Worst were the negative, furtive reactions of those who considered people from the Caribbean French "in spite of everything," whereas Arabs…

We slowly acclimatized. Below our building there was a handball court, and Zacarias made a beeline for it. But the neighborhood kids had their habits, and weren't prepared to welcome a newcomer just like that—even less such a good player. I followed Zac onto the court and, needless to say, we won more or less every game. But we didn't necessarily win the fights that broke out. Here too there were large families, but Zacarias and I were older, so calling our sisters to our defense was out of the question. The brawls were more violent than they had been in Alsace.

It was a good two years before we felt at home in the south. In the Razimbaud projects the older boys were really tough. Each building had its gang and gang leader. For months, it was impossible for us to join one of the gangs. And without a gang it was hard to be accepted in the neighborhood. A few weeks before our arrival in Narbonne, a dozen or so young guys from the neighborhood, aged fifteen to twenty-three, raped a young woman on the beach after beating up her husband. A few of them were arrested and put in jail; others fled the country. Several families in Razimbaud were strongly implicated, to a greater or lesser degree, in this ugly incident. When we arrived, the projects were still abuzz over this painful affair, and the overall climate was heavy.

Families from all over North Africa as well as native French families lived in our building. This was in contrast to the neighboring Pastouret projects, where pretty much only people of French origin lived. There was a bitter rivalry between Pastouret and Razimbaud. Pastouret was the "fascist" projects, and Razimbaud the melting-pot. Another community, St. Jean-St. Pierre, likewise forgotten by liberals who sleep well at night, was more or less exclusively inhabited by North Africans and Turks. Depending on the day, and the mood, gangs from St. Jean-St. Pierre would either support or attack us. One thing was sure, however: whatever disagreements might break out between Razimbaud and St. Jean-St. Pierre, the two neighborhoods were united against Pastouret, the fascists' domain. The honor of the Arabs ("Arabs" meaning, in this case, all the inhabitants of a neighborhood) was safe and sound.

Thirteen and fourteen years old respectively, Zacarias and I were content to stand on the sidelines and observe. We didn't take part in the really serious fights—except for one unforgettable time. There was a big party at Razimbaud, and the kids from St. Jean-St. Pierre, who hadn't been invited, wanted in. The whole scene quickly degenerated into battle, right in the middle of the street. Thirty young people mixing it up. Zac and I managed to be in the thick of it without taking any nasty knocks. We were hidden behind two huge bruisers from our projects and as soon as they pinned an enemy to the ground, we'd leap on him, while the two guys, who were built like tanks, went about the business of bringing in the next customer.

In that kind of neighborhood, there was just one simple rule: unless you were feared, you were nothing. So the aim was to make people afraid of you as a matter of practice. And things happened fast. After two years, Zacarias and I also had learned how to make people respect us. There was a group of about fifteen kids whose families had moved into the apartment block at the same time, and we formed our own gang. Among the newcomers were two burly brothers from Northern France who, like us, had an accent you could cut with a knife.

Our buddy Jacques lived just below us. His family was very hospitable and we made the most of it. His mother was a politically committed woman, a trade unionist. We could talk for hours on end with her about politics, society and the future. Jacques's father was a sales rep for a coffee company. So in their house, there was always room at the table and coffee was always brewing. Whenever we could, several times a day, Zac and I went downstairs to see them. Sometimes we returned home only to sleep, sometimes not even then. For us, that family was a "real" family, warm and noisy, with laughter rather than shouting. During the 1982 World Cup we more or less moved in with them. That was a real party. Jacques's family had a soft spot for Zacarias in particular. For them he was the neighborhood mascot. In fact, Zac could really lay on the charm; his kindness, subtlety, thoughtfulness, and wit won many a heart. And above all he liked helping out people he appreciated.

In our apartment block, there was also a "bike specialist" named Jean. He would steal bicycle and motorcycle parts and use them to assemble his own machines. That's how we got to know him—he walked off with the derailleur from my bike. I recognized it at once outside his garage, because I had put my own mark on it. So I took Zacarias and went to see Jean, and ordered him to give back the derailleur. He was a good sport. He let me have it back and we became friends.

Jean had a brother and two half-brothers, really big guys who became our "insurance policy" in the neighborhood. Jean and his brothers took over several unused cellars in our building, filling them with long rows of bikes and spare parts. They had all the latest gear, derailleurs as well as revolutionary tire pumps, the mud guards of the future... Sometimes Zacarias and I would join them on their Saturday afternoon bike rides. We would go as far as one hundred miles and return home exhausted. For two days afterwards we would be unable to walk, but they were back on the road the very next day.

The bike thieves introduced us to other thieves, including Dave, the resident daredevil, who was my age. He was an orphan, his parents had died in a car crash. His grandmother did her honest best to bring him up. His uncle, a petty thief who was in Carcassonne jail at the time, was something of a hero to his nephew. With a family like that, Dave didn't go unnoticed in the neighborhood. He spent most of his time breaking into pay phones, or stealing bikes and motorbikes and cars: anything he could get his hands on. He also launched a stock-car craze—with other people's cars. At fourteen, he was stealing top-of-the-line Citroëns, as well as cheaper models. One day he gave the cops the slip in the projects; he knew every nook and cranny. Dave was definitely something of a neighborhood hero.

But mostly we kept our distance from the thieves, including Dave. Maybe because of our old orphanage days, we mistrusted the kids there who were brought up badly, or rather not brought up at all: future delinquents. It was Dave who told us you could go to jail for thievery starting at age thirteen. We took the warning to heart, even if it didn't deter him. Neither Zacarias nor I made much of a hoodlum. We were too scared of not being able to study because of a criminal record. If there was one thing we were really sure about, it was that we wanted to go to university.

Zacarias in particular was possessed by a fear of delinquency. He warned me about spending time in the "bad company" of the gangs and advised me to be careful not to get mixed up in any shady business.

We did pretty well at school, without much effort. But as Zac and I enjoyed more or less total freedom at home, in class we weren't exactly models of good behavior. One year I racked up about sixty hours of detention and was expelled. So we ended up at the Jules Ferry secondary school, on the other side of town. It took us up to forty-five minutes to get there on foot. It was completely different from Montesquieu, more upper-crust. The beautiful, well-maintained school buildings encircled a large, green expanse. The day-to-day reality of the place was not quite what it seemed, however. Weapons would make the rounds—knives, coshes and even, on one occasion, a revolver. There were lots of fights. I moved up into the third year, but my marks were average, not nearly as good as in my second year. And I was undisciplined as ever. The math teacher took an instant disliking to me. Zacarias, who was still in the second year, was craftier than I; he realized that it paid to keep a low profile.

One afternoon, I sprained my thumb playing handball in the yard. It hurt and I wanted to go home. Because the supervisor refused, I made as if to force my way past him. A school counselor who happened to be there tried to restrain me by pulling on my sprained thumb. A sharp pain shot up my arm and my reflex was to push him hard. Unfortunately, he fell to the ground. The counselor was beside himself and told me to get in his car, saying, "We're going to go and see your father!"

That year my father had in fact settled in Narbonne. Things were better between us; we no longer ran away as soon as we saw him. He had a small company and worked on building sites. He lived in a shabby two-room apartment, but drove around in a Mercedes.

The school counselor made me get into his car and we found my father at the building site. Needless to say, I wasn't very proud of myself, even if I reckoned I was in the right. When we got there, my father was in the middle of replastering the front a three-story building. He was perched up a ladder, with two bags of cement propped on his left shoulder. The counselor stopped the car for a few seconds. He looked at my father on the ladder with his bags of cement, then suddenly changed his mind. "We're going back to school!" he exclaimed. When we got back, he dismissed me, saying, "It's okay, you can go back to class." I was flabbergasted. A faint smile played on his lips. I should have suspected that he had something in mind, but at that moment, I was just taken aback.

I realized only later what his plan was. Too late. At the end of the school year, the counselor put together a vocational file for me. Instead of moving up to the fourth year, I ended up in a vocational training school. I took it as an act of personal vengeance, all the more so because nobody had warned me; I wasn't informed until the end of summer holidays. When the day came to go back to school, I turned up at Jules Ferry as usual, only to be turned away by a supervisor. He told me that I was no longer enrolled at the school, that I was now enrolled at the Jean Moulin vocational college, in plumbing. I realized that I'd been had, and I was now careering along at high speed in the slow lane.

As for Zacarias, he was in third year. But he was furious about that scheming school counselor. We were by then convinced of three kinds of bigotry in the state education system. One had to do with the color of your skin, another was linked to your cultural origins, and the third was to do with social class. Zacarias was schocked by the career path that had been foisted on me, possibly even more disgusted than I was. From then on, he was suspicious of everybody in the state system. The betrayal of his brother's trust put an end to his own. So as not to give the system the slightest chance of jerking him around, he started to work hard and behave himself.

In our neighborhood there was a mini-market which was habitually robbed. One or two young guys would wedge one of the windows open, and then pay a little nighttime visit to the candy store. One of the cellars under their building was filled with candy. Once I found myself looking at a mound of Mars bars, Kit Kats, Mounds bars and the like, hoarded for house parties. During school holidays we would spend whole days "defending the walls of the neighborhood," and hanging out in stairways. Some guys drank beer, others smoked joints. But that wasn't really our thing, Zac's and mine. He didn't even smoke cigarettes. I had the odd puff, but only to be like my buddies.

At secondary school, Zacarias gave up handball completely. He enrolled in a club when we arrived in Narbonne, but came back from the first training session saying that the level of play was low, and that he wasn't going to waste his time with those people. The coach even came to our home to try to change his mind. But he was wasting his time, because when my brother makes up his mind… He was very ambitious, very demanding, extreme. With my brother, it's all or nothing. When he believes in something, he does everything in his powers to reach his goal. But if he's disappointed, it's all over, and he draws the line from one day to the next.

Later on he half-tried to get involved in rugby by joining the Narbonne Racing Club, then the French champions. He played on the wing and played well. He trained for two seasons and then complained about some coaches being racists. My brother said that even if Arabs were good, they weren't selected for the team. According to Zacarias the rugby world in Narbonne was full of fascists. He explained to me that for the rugby players he knew, a "good Arab" was one they could go on a bar crawl with, and then smash his face in at the end of the binge.

A year went by in my new school. Zacarias was fifteen. The third-year class marked another turning point for him because he switched social circles, making some good friends. At Jules Ferry he met middle-class children, children of managers and teachers, brought up with their futures all mapped out, right through university. On holidays these kids were taken to the four corners of the earth. Did Zacarias suffer by living among them, without the same opportunities? Doubtless he did, but it was all in silence. In any event, it was during those years that he forged his closest friendships, with Yves, who would "naturally" take over his father's business, and Maurice, whose father was a property developer.

Right up until he started to go off-track, Zacarias stayed very close to these friends. The last person in his group to see him in France was Yves, with whom he drank a few beers when he passed through in 1997. Early in their friendship, Yves had set up a billiard room and a discothèque in his basement. Zacarias hung out there all the time. From time to time, my brother's buddies invited me to their homes. One of them, whose father owned a plumbing company, had an indoor swimming pool. Spending time with those particular people, at that particular time, that my brother realized the power of money. It was a turning point for him.

At the end of his fourth year, he did something that surprised me.

He requested transfer to a vocational school, to earn certification as a mechanic and fitter. Was he suffering from an inferiority complex? Or was he trying to follow my lead? Finally I realized that he was humiliated by his social roots. The son of a Moroccan cleaning woman, in the midst of sons of company directors? The La Croix secondary school, where he would have done his fifth year, had a reputation in our neighborhood as solidly middle-class. Among its pupils were said to be some little fascists. I don't know if this was true, but for my brother "middle class" meant "not like me." A school where you had to wear the latest fashion, sport Nikes and have a name-brand backpack. Impossible! Zacarias finally explained his choice to me with the pithy complaint: "I was all on my own." On his own socially? All his friends were certainly moving up into the fifth year at La Croix. But who among them was able to share his unease? If I had been at La Croix, he probably would have stuck with it, because when the hard knocks came, there would have been the two of us.

In spite of everything, I tried to make him change his mind. I explained to him that the vocational school was the very opposite of the fast track, and that he was the only one of us who could succeed with flying colors. Even if it was hard at the outset, he would have to grit his teeth, knock a few heads together, and everything would be fine. But was I persuasive enough? Deep down, I knew perfectly well that he was right, that he would never really feel like the others, because he really wasn't like them. Our mother wasn't much help. She would repeat to him, as she did to me, "Choose what you want, I trust you. In any event, don't dream, I don't have the money to pay for your studies, you'll have to work."

Unwittingly, I probably influenced Zacarias's drift toward a technical training certificate. Aware of having been steered into what some regarded as a dead end, where people accepted what was in store for them without their heart being in it, I started to study very seriously, first to get my vocational diploma and then to go for my advanced vocational diploma. And I realized at the end of the day that the workshop, where you learn practical things, like working copper, steel, and lead, gave me a lot of satisfaction. I came into contact with enthusiastic teachers who encouraged pride in a job well done. As a result, when I discussed day-to-day life at the vocational school with Zacarias, I projected an image of fulfillment which was much more appealing than a difficult baccalaureate from a middle-class secondary school, unlikely to be followed by university studies.

So he switched schools. In no time he realized that he'd made a mistake. The students were not there because they wanted to be, but because they had no choice. They had been labelled "bad," and pushed down a dead end. Zacarias couldn't stand it. His self-esteem took a dive.

As the years passed my sister Nadia grew further and further away from the family unit, the flipside, perhaps, of her compulsory devotion to us when we were very small. To my mother, Nadia was an artist. She did the general baccalaureate and got excellent grades but, encouraged by our mother, she dropped her studies and enrolled at the Perpignan Drama School. Convinced that her daughter would become a star, my frugal mother even rented a small apartment for her.

The teachers, the headmaster, and even the social worker at the secondary school tried to convince my mother and my sister that they were making a big mistake. They came to our home to talk about it. But nothing could change my mother's mind. She would say to anybody who would listen that her daughter was an artist, a future star, that her name would be in lights. Indeed our name would be famous, much later on—alas.

Nadia came home only occasionally. This elevated her status even further, as the prodigal child. Imagine what it was like for my mother to see her daughter on the road to fame and fortune. Nadia wasn't a bad actress, and she went off to Paris to attend another drama school.

Zacarias and I did our best to stay out of it. Of course, we lived in the same apartment as my mother, our stepfather and our sisters. Mornings, we would see them at breakfast; evenings, at supper; and sometimes right after school, before we met up with our friends. But we didn't feel that we belonged to the family. The idea of "home" was vague. We lived under the same roof, we depended on our mother to eat, but we stubbornly refused to depend on her for anything else, especially affection. To avoid arguments, we avoided discussion with her, when we could.

My mother was a mercurial individual. She lost her temper easily, and sometimes turned violent. So it was better to give her the least possible provocation. As I've said, Jamila bore the brunt of it. Once a pretty girl, small and delicate, she became bulimic, then started to put on weight. At meals, my mother would bombard her with criticism. In the middle of eating she would relentlessly reproach her, sometimes even in the presence of strangers. Depending on her mood, my sister would either ignore my mother, or answer back; when she did answer back, it was sure to end in shouts and sobs.

Jamila's behavior become weirder and weirder. She would sometimes wander outside at night, and she was assaulted more than once. She ended up going to see a social worker to try to get a place in a hostel. My mother met the social worker. She told us she had explained that her daughter wanted to leave home so that she could hang out in the streets and have fun. Aïcha told the social worker that she loved her daughter, that she didn't want her to go away, that she was worried about her, and that if she came back, everything would be all right. The social worker, and then even Jamila, believed it. Jamila came home. And before long, the old habits crept back. My mother criticized the way Jamila behaved; Jamila was always the "bad seed."

Zacarias and I had to butt in now and then, even if it didn't do any good. We urged our mother: "Stop, Mum, why are you talking to her like that, stop!" She made as if she couldn't hear us. Our stepfather, for his part, was a mere shadow. But our father was getting closer to us. Our mother's strategy toward him had changed. She no longer banned us from seeing him, on the contrary, she would say, "Go on, go out with him, make him pay!" Our father lived hand-to-mouth, and when he did have money, was very generous to those around him. But it seemed never to occur to him to give our mother the slightest allowance.

In any event, Zacarias and I decided we would see him regularly. We were fond of him. We didn't really feel the fondness of sons, because he hadn't raised us. But if he had been absent, at least he'd never been mean. He'd never hit us. And for us, that was very important. What we really felt for him was sympathy. He was kind to us, he gave us a bit of money. And he was funny. He was a little wild; he had lots of affairs and he even took us to discothèques. One summer day, just before school started again, he really surprised us. Zacarias and I bumped into him on the Cours Gambetta, beside the canal, a pleasant spot. We walked with him. He was nattily dressed, wearing a suit and tie, and told us that he had come to live in Narbonne so that he could see us regularly. As we talked, we walked past a developer's office, and our father said, "Come with me, I'll show you how you find work when you're really looking for it!" He walked into the office, said hello to the staff, introduced himself as a contractor, and asked to see the person running the agency, who, as luck would have it, was available. Then we discovered a facet of our father that we'd never seen: he was a self-confident man, sure of his professional worth. He was carrying a small black briefcase from which he took out some photos of his projects—a press book, no less. He told the agency boss what he could do, listed his job experience, told him that he'd just arrived in Narbonne. He was his own best salesman, and things fell into place.

A while later, our father was driving a lorry on which was written, in large blue letters, "Entreprise Moussaoui." With his direct way of doing things, he had secured several jobs. He had bought his equipment and signed up workers. So we saw our father as a resourceful man who earned a good living because he was hard-working, organized and well-regarded in his profession. A few years later, we were brought down to earth.

Our father had once again disappeared, a few months earlier. Then one day, walking toward the Narbonne city hall, a smiling man stopped us in the streets: "Aren't you the Moussaoui boys?" We did actually look a lot like our father. So we nodded, regarding him with curiosity and suspicion.

"I knew it was you! I know your father!" exclaimed the stranger, breaking into a broad smile.

"Really? You know our father?"

"I'll say! I was in prison with him! I've just got out!"

At first my brother and I didn't react, except to cast an eye around to make sure that nobody had heard, especially no buddies. Once we'd got over our surprise, we started asking the stranger some questions. The stranger told us some very complicated story about money, and that our father was in good health. "He's in good shape, he's a brave guy, and he doesn't get upset about things." We figured that he wouldn't be particularly intimidated by the other inmates. Once in Mulhouse we had seen a man attack him with a knife. He grabbed the weapon with his bare hands, broke the blade, and proceeded to smash up the other man's face.

Back home, we said nothing about what we learned. Not that we took it too seriously. For us, it was just another chance to have a laugh. When we squabbled, one of us would always whisper to the other, with a big smile, "Watch out, or I'll tell everyone you're the son of a jailbird!"

About that time our mother and stepfather bought a corner grocery, for next to nothing, in an urban-renewal area near the center of Narbonne. It took off in no time, primarily because the whole block was being renovated. With her innate business sense, my mother had been clever enough to stay a step ahead of the developers. Later she resold the business and made a pretty profit, enough to buy a plot of land at Roche-Grise, a fairly sought-after area on the edge of Narbonne. With a small loan the two began building a large house.

Zac and I were happy at the prospect of leaving Razimbaud, with all its petty crime, and the stigma you couldn't shake. Saïd built the house himself, taking on two laborers to help him, and getting Zacarias and me to help out on weekends and school holidays. We poured cement, mixed plaster, laid concrete block, dug the foundation, put up the supporting walls in the basement, laid floors, laid brick, helped to install the frame—we worked non-stop. Our mother appointed herself site forewoman. She didn't know a thing about it, but she was very good at information-gathering. She spent her time visiting colleagues who had had their houses built, architects to ask for hints and tips, and builders she knew to glean advice. She repeated over and over to Saïd, whenever he had a suggestion of his own, "It's my house!" Thanks to all of us, "her" house was built in three months. Saïd probably thought that it would also be "his" house. He was wrong.

Aïcha said she didn't have enough money to install central heating, so the whole house was fitted with electric heaters. We moved in in September, even as the last brush of paint was drying, and when the first cold snap arrived, the plaster still was not completely dry. Moisture oozed from every wall. Needless to say, the first electricity bills were huge. Our mother tore out her hair, bawled at us, accused us of deliberately wasting electricity, and endlessly told us that we were eating away at all her savings. As we well knew, my mother counted every penny. When she was young, this "sense of economy" was probably logical enough. But it had gotten to the point where money was the only thing that mattered.

Our sisters were accused of far worse than profligacy, such as of being too close to our stepfather. He would sigh and wearily shrug his shoulders. As was his wont, he never said anything. We just thought he was weak. In reality, as we later realized, he had been biding his time. He had another woman who lived near the grocery, even had a child with her. One day, quietly as ever, he announced as much to my mother, and left her.

After Saïd left, we bumped into him from time to time, and our contacts were friendly. He had never done us any harm, really we rather liked him, even if neither party had ever put much into the relationship. With Saïd gone, our mother met a few other men, about whom, unfortunately, we knew absolutely nothing.

We spent the whole of the following summer at Roche-Grise. It was a residential neighborhood for architects, engineers and civil servants. Many of our neighbors had swimming pools and tennis courts; some even had horses. We were the only North Africans in the area, and we didn't make any outward show of wealth, but our mother, a cleaning woman, had succeeded in having her own house built there. It was a substantial climb up the social ladder.

Roche-Grise had a camping site equipped with a foosball table and a ping-pong table, so the summer was anything but boring. It didn't take long for us to get together with others our age. We went from one swimming pool to the next, tried our hand at tennis, and even, sometimes, got to ride ponies—all thanks to Zacarias. Because he was quickly accepted in this circle. My brother was smart, fun to be around, quick-witted, and a charmer. His sense of humor, which was sometimes scathing, could get people laughing until they cried. Those who took a dim view of the Moroccan sons of a cleaning woman invading the middle class circle—and there were some— mostly kept it to themselves. We were athletic, and Razimbaud had taught us to use our fists, which wasn't necessarily the way the middle class went about things.

Tennis was a way to get your foot in the door in our neighborhood. Zacarias, who had never played before, quickly got the hang of it. So he became an acceptable partner, his first "in." And, among our neighbors, there were, of course, girls.

Her name was Fanny. A pretty blond, with white skin and pale eyes. She lived two hundred yards from our house. Her brother was one of my friends. Zacarias met her at a neighbor's house, at their pool. She was fifteen, like him. It was the start of a real love story, a story that lasted ten years. What Zacarias could not find in his own home he tried to construct elsewhere. He was looking for harmony, gentleness, affection, honesty, loyalty, integrity—in short, emotional security. He found it with Fanny.

True, my brother was secretive and modest by nature. But little by little he told Fanny about his pain and suffering, and about the permanent tension at home with mother. Fanny was his secret garden. He never talked about her, but he spent nearly all his time with her. The only problem was that Fanny came from a "good family." A "good family" that didn't look too kindly on her new friends— and boyfriend. Her father was a high-up in a big company. He drove a sports car. Her mother was a civil servant. They had a pool, too. Fanny's father was racist, in a distressingly predictable way. Fanny's mother knew that her daughter was dating my brother; to start with she didn't say anything. But when her husband found out, she closed ranks with him, and they called Fanny's friendship "disgraceful." When Zacarias was just a friend among a bunch of friends, he was OK. Now he was dangerous, a threat to their daughter.

At the time, as he liked to put it, Zacarias was a "salmon"—swimming upstream, from the vocational diploma to the baccalaureate, and from the baccalaureate to the advanced vocational certificate. And despite the whirlpools, he got there. So he had every reason to be proud of himself. But his girlfriend's parents didn't see things quite the same way. At first, Zacarias did his best to please them. Like me, he thought some people were racists more because of a lack of culture, or out of fear rather than from basic malevolence. As a result, Zac thought Fanny's parents could probably be "educated." He thought that once they got to know him, all the barriers and prejudices against him would come tumbling down. It was a charitable way of looking at things—and way off-mark. He was always polite and smiling, but it didn't alter Fanny's parents' feelings one iota: their daughter deserved better than an Arab. And Fanny probably made the mistake of being too honest in telling Zacarias what her parents said about him. My brother eventually decided that they had a basic lack of intelligence, that no matter what he did, Fanny's parents would never change their views. Zacarias started to view them with contempt. He didn't make an effort to be polite anymore, and he didn't conceal from them his new attitude. When he went to pick Fanny up for a date, he didn't even go up to the door; instead he stayed on the street. Actually, that probably suited them fine. As for our mother, Zacarias kept her as far away as he could from his emotional life. He brought Fanny home only when he was absolutely sure that mother was out.

As the years passed things between Zacarias and Aïcha just got worse. I managed to listen to our mother, bide my time, and let the storm pass when shouts and screams filled the house. I had a soft spot for her, figuring that her tiring and sometimes demeaning job was the main cause of her exhaustion and irritability.

Zacarias, though, seemed to have run out of patience completely. He now refused to make any compromises. He was more pig-headed than I. For him, holding one's tongue for the sake of peace amounted to cowardice. From age fourteen on, he didn't let our mother get away with anything—particularly when he saw her quarrelling with Jamila. One day he sat down opposite me in our bedroom, head in his hands, and told me wearily that he could no longer stand the terrible arguments that rocked the house.

He became cold and clinical. I think he stopped feeling any love for her. He was hard on her. He referred to her as "that woman." When they had rows, it was heavy. Zacarias reproached her for living in a fantasy world. The more she lost her temper, the more he made it a point of honor to stay very cool, very cold. That unsettled Aïcha and he knew it only too well. She would shout louder and louder. He was like marble, staring straight at her and answering, "It's not true. You're lying. You're making the whole thing up."

I reckoned that it served no purpose to put up such resistance, to play power games with her. She would never countenance any opinion but her own. So what was the point? Nothing would get her to back down. My tactic, to keep the house from turning into a battlefield every day, was to let her shout, saying nothing in reply; I would listen to her until her anger had subsided. Only when she had calmed down would I try to reason with her. I tried to persuade Zacarias to do the same. He would hear me out, but even when he tried not to argue, she provoked him so much that eventually he rose to the bait. My mother's philosophy was never to settle things.

I know that these accusations levelled at my mother may seem serious, but they are what really went on. She said violent things. When he heard them, Zacarias would clench his fists and desperately try to keep his cool. It was hard. The shouting would go on for hours. A row between my mother and my little brother might start at six P.M. and go on until two in the morning. My mother gave up only when she saw her son completely at the end of his tether, about to break down. Once he turned away from her, he would explode. Sobbing, usually. But never in front of her. I told him the same thing every time: "You mustn't get into these states. She's our mother, and you can see she's not well. She's tired, too; her work's tiring…"

The story of the council grants is typical. Zacarias and I both received study grants from the Aude council. They were meant to cover the cost of transportation to and from school. The money came to our mother, who was supposed to pass it along to us each month. But she said we cost her too much money, all told, so she didn't have to give us the bus money. She would either say "Sort it out for yourselves," or "I've already given you the money."

"How are we supposed to get to school?"

"I've already given you the money."

"No you haven't! Give us the money, it's not your money."

"No I won't! You're liars, you've already spent the money, I gave it to you already."

Result: we found ways to take the bus money—our money—from her purse. We didn't have a choice. We had to be at school by eight o'clock and lived four miles away. We tried hitch-hiking several times, but it only worked now and then; sometimes we got a ride straight away, but most of the time we were stuck on the roadside, thumbs in the air. Who, on the way to work at seven in the morning, would pick up two dark-skinned lads? And then in the evening it was the same story. For a long time I let it all wash over me. And for a long time Zacarias put up with things, too, but there was one time when Aïcha played what my brother called a "real dirty trick" on him. And the row they had was more violent than any before.

It was the day Zacarias was to take his practical exam for the vocational diploma. He had to be at school by 7:30 A.M. for registration. But the bus didn't come that early. So Zacarias asked our mother to drive him, and she agreed. On the fateful day, Zacarias got up early and got himself ready. Not a sound in the house. After a while, seeing what time it was, he went and knocked on our mother's bedroom door. No answer. He knocked louder, and called her name. Nothing. He went in. Aïcha opened an eye. He said to her, "Mum, hurry up, I'm going to be late." She looked at him and said, "I'm tired. Get yourself to school. Let me sleep." And she turned to the wall. He went on at her. She screamed at him, "Get yourself to school, leave me in peace!" Zacarias was beside himself. He flew out of the house, slamming every door, hitchhiked and got to school forty-five minutes late. At the end of the exam he still hadn't finished his paper. In a fit, he chucked it into the wastebasket. A teacher took pity on him, retrieved his exam paper and handed it in. Thanks to him, Zacarias got his diploma.

He never forgave our mother for what she did that day. He was forever saying, "I knew she wouldn't do a thing to help me, but I didn't know she was capable of doing something to hurt me." Every time they argued, the violence of their words just got worse and worse. Zacarias would get pale in the face, but he snapped back at everything she said. He was in control of himself, but maybe he would crack? That's what it looked like, if the expression on his face was anything to go by.

One day, during one of those fights, I had to intervene to stop him from hitting her. That was it. I advised him to leave home before he really lost it: "You've got to go, bro. I'll find a solution for you." I asked a friend who lived in the middle of Narbonne to put him up for awhile. So Zacarias left home one morning in 1986. It was meant to be forever. He returned briefly in 1988, then left again. After that he didn't return until 1996, eight years later. His head was shaved, and he had a long beard and wore short pants. According to my mother, he'd come to ask her forgiveness.

3

LOOKING FOR AN IDENTITY

At home, Aïcha never spoke to us in Arabic. So we felt out of place even among North Africans, not knowing their language. When we asked our mother to teach us a few words, she would laugh at our accent and our lousy pronunciation—so we stopped asking. Our sisters, of course, were born in Morocco and went back there almost every year—they spoke Arabic. But when Zac and I met Moroccan families, they would feel sorry for us. "Oh, they don't speak Arabic? *Meskeen!* Poor things!" And my mother would respond, "No they don't, they're right little French boys, those two."

Neither did our mother teach us about Arab ways and customs, or about Muslim culture. Not because she wasn't acquainted with that culture, but because she didn't want to teach us. She was quoted recently as saying, "I made sure they didn't hang out with Arabs."* Zac and I asked her several times how you prayed and why. She dodged the question. She told us it wasn't what people of our age did. Yet, since Mulhouse, we'd seen our friends going to the mosque with their fathers. So why not us? We felt ridiculous in the company of others. Who might have told us all about these things?

---

* *Le Monde,* 27 September 2001.

Not our father, who wasn't a practising Muslim, even if he had been around. Not our aunts and uncles, who all lived on the other side of the Mediterranean. So we decided to ask Saïd, our mother's partner, who was a practising Muslim.

We saw him bowing, getting up, and kneeling back down again. We wanted to know what it all meant, what was the meaning of the words he uttered. In a kind, if slightly awkward, way he gave us the relevant books, not knowing how to explain it all himself. We didn't understand the first thing about it. The books explained in concrete terms how to pray, but didn't give us any spiritual information. There wasn't a mosque in Narbonne. There was a prayer hall at St. Jean-St. Pierre, but I didn't know that until much later. Like lots of prayer halls, there was no sign on the street. It was discreet, in an ordinary apartment.

There was no way that we could ask our North African friends anything, because that would expose our terrible lack of culture, and they would have really teased us. Zac and I met discouragement at every turn, until we gave up our quest. I was twenty-one when I went into a mosque for the first time, in Montpellier. I think the first mosque Zacarias entered was in Great Britain. I believe that this religious ignorance has had a huge impact on his life, and that the same is true for people drawn to the al-Qaeda training camps in Pakistan, and for French prisoners at Guantanamo Bay.

At this juncture, I'd like to interrupt my story and say one or two things which seem crucial to any understanding of Zacarias' subsequent actions.

There are now more than one billion people in the world who adhere to Islam. Ninety-five percent of them are Sunnis. Four percent are Shi'ites. Slightly more than a million are Wahhabi, but this particular million is disproportionately wealthy, because

Wahhabism is the state religious ideology of Saudi Arabia, which possesses the world's largest confirmed oil reserves.*

Part of the appeal of Wahhabism is that it offers a reply to international horrors. The state of the world is disturbing, with the war in Chechnya and its appalling massacres, or the fallout of the war waged by the Russians in Afghanistan. (Zacarias and I felt tremendous admiration for the late Shah Ahmad Massoud, a hero of the war with Russia who would later lead the "Northern Alliance" against the Taliban.) Bosnia underwent ethnic cleansing, which Zac and I saw as a systematic extermination, genocide taking place before our very eyes. And then there is Algeria, something of a special case in the litany of bloodshed: more than 100,000 dead in ten years. A civilian population massacred. Last, Palestine is under occupation. The Palestinians live under a system of apartheid.

For any young North African living in France, all this horror is intolerable and exacerbates feelings that are already greatly bruised by overtly expressed discrimination against Arabs and Muslims. We are actually easy prey to bigots because our vulnerability is well-known. No voices are being raised to give vent to or to defend our feelings. One-track thinking rules, and nobody dares speak out.

In Montpellier, Zacarias made friends with students who came from a tough neighborhood called Petit-Bard, and from the Paillade projects. These students explained to him that what was going on in Algeria was a legitimate struggle against corrupt leaders and injustices, and that the fighters in this struggle were called the *mujaheddin*. Their analysis seemed very odd to us: Algeria being a land of Islam, how could you make war in the name of Islam against other Muslims? Women, children, young men and old, beheaded with

---

* These numbers on the branches of Islam are the subject of debate. In particular, some estimates of the number of Wahhabi adherents are five or even ten times greater.

axes, throats slit with saws! That couldn't have been done in the name of Islam. All these atrocities were to be condemned in no uncertain terms.

Nowadays in France, when a young Muslim becomes interested in learning about his religion, wants to find out about his parents' values and the history of the community, and his parents can't provide answers, he is likely to turn to a cultural or religious association. He goes to Arab-Muslim bookshops, as well as traditional bookshops. In the latter, the material is often quite expensive, and geared to an intellectual readership. Furthermore, the books are often written by Orientalists. The Arab-Muslim bookshops tend to be friendlier and more easy-going, and less expensive. You can find plenty of things evoking your parents' culture: the same perfume; the same clothes; *soubhahs* and *siwaks;** magazines; tapes and videos for learning Arabic; the Koran; and books about the foundations of Islam, religious practices, the history of the Arab world, and Arab-Muslim culture. Books of every shape and size.

The young Muslim may also be approached by *tablighs,†* whom you can meet by chance in markets. He might attend the fair organized by the French Union of Islamic Organizations [UOIF]. There he will find all kinds of products: clothes, perfumes—anything and everything that can be traded. Or he might sign up for a religious course conducted by the Association of Islamic Welfare Projects in France [APBIF], which also organizes religious festivals, such as the commemoration of the birth of the Prophet Muhammad [ﷺ]. The landscape for a young novice is like rich, uncultivated terrain. His first steps are haphazard. During religious meetings, people may

---

* *Soubhahs:* prayer beads. A *siwak* is a wooden twig that is used to clean your teeth. It may be from an olive or palm tree, but the best *siwaks* come from the arak tree.

† Members of a pietistic movement founded in 1927; by nature it is missionary, proselytizing and radically anti-fundamentalist.

bring up trivial or secondary subjects year after year, making others think that they are the crucial questions. Quite by chance the novice may stumble upon an extremely vitriolic book, or an especially understated book. He may find authentic religious instruction—or political and sectarian indoctrination.

In the absence of any informed parental authority or clearly defined religious authority, the young novice is left to his own devices. And danger lurks everywhere. A lot of those talking in the name of religion are in no way qualified to do so. The main criteria for imams are quite simply knowledge of Arabic, and an ability to step up into the *minbar,* or pulpit, to speak. (Sometimes imams are required to know the Koran by heart, but no-one ever asks any questions about the real nature of their theological studies.) The first generation of immigrants had two concerns: finding places of worship, and having someone available to teach Arabic and the Koran to their children. But when those entrusted with these responsibilities are novices, there is no telling what education they might provide.

Young students who call themselves members of the Muslim Brotherhood, *Hizb ut-Tahrir* (the Party of Liberation), or Wahhabis are fierce rivals to this generation of imams. The young students run associations that organize Arabic lessons, tutoring and religious instruction. Sometimes they even work from the inside, at first assisting the imams, and gradually taking over the role of educator for children and young people. These young students thus manage to be in contact with the young members of the second generation of immigrants. Hitherto, serious and moderate traditional religious instruction has been almost nonexistent.

Certain authors come up again and again: Sayyid Qutb, Abul Ala Mawdudi, Yusuf Al-Qaradawi, Muhammad ibn Abd Al-Wahhab, Ibn Baz, 'Abd ul-Aziz Al-Uthaymeen—all leading figures of

Wahhabism and the Muslim Brotherhood, also known as Qutbists. What do they write? One or two selected excerpts from Sayyid Qutb (1906–1966) may be instructive:

> Today, a Muslim society no longer exists, there is no more Islam and there are no more Muslims.... Muslim society will only come back into being when existing regimes have been destroyed, and given way to a power which respects divine legislation to the letter.... All the societies in the world, with no exceptions, are idolatrous and full of infidels, conscious that authority belongs solely to God. For when a man dares to invent laws, he proclaims himself the equal of God. And all peoples which subject themselves to such a man without resistance or rebellion are in a state of adoration of him, by their obedience to him [...]. The true Muslim today is the Muslim who makes *jihad* against all governments whose legislation is human in origin, in order to topple them and reinstate divine legislation.*

From another book:

> There is but one house, it is the house of Islam which contains the Muslim state, any other house [where this authority is non-existent, which is the case everywhere, even in Islamic lands]† is merely hostility for the Muslim and his relationship with it must only be war or else an

---

* Sayyid Qutb, *A l'ombre du Qour'an (In the Shade of the Koran)*, Al-Hidayah Al-Islamiyah, 1988.

† Author's note.

armistice with special conditions; it can hardly be regarded as the house of Islam and there can be no friendly understanding between its inhabitants and Muslims.*

Hatred oozes from every page. These statements are the manifestation of an embittered and even sectarian state of mind, and they are accordingly dangerous.

One of the key figures of Wahhabism and Qutbism is Ayman Az-Zawahiri. Who is this Egyptian, known as Osama bin Laden's right-hand man? He came into the public eye when he appeared with bin Laden in one or two videos broadcast by Al-Jazeera. He was arrested and imprisoned in 1981 following the assassination of the Egyptian president Anwar es-Sadat. Since 1991 he has been the leader of the Egyptian organization Islamic Jihad, thought to be one of the most extremist and murderous groups. In fact, in 1992 alone, Islamic Jihad's terrorist operations were responsible for the deaths of 1,200 people in Egypt. You recognize a tree by its fruit! What does Ayman Az-Zawahiri say about the writings of Sayyid Qutb?

> With the execution of the most important of the Muslim Brotherhood leaders, Sayyid Qutb, the powers-that-be thought that they had managed to rid Egypt of the Islamic movement. But that act was the detonator that sparked the Jihadist movement against the Egyptian government.... Sayyid Qutb made possible the establishment of the Brotherhood in his explosive book *Milestones on the Road*, which gave rise to the revival of fundamentalism.... The group that had been led by Sayyid Qutb decided to aim its

---

* Sayyid Qutb, *Jalons sur la route de l'islam (Milestones on the Road)*, Imprimerie de Carthage, 1968.

attacks against the powers then in place, because these powers were the enemy of Islam and had strayed from the way approved by Allah in refusing to comply with his Law. Sayyid Qutb's call was—and is—the spark fuelling the Islamic revolution against the enemies of Islam both within and without, and bloody episodes occurred day after day. This revolution assumed a greater resolve in its belief, a refined precision in its strategy, a richer understanding of the nature of the struggle, and more experience in relation to the obstacles encountered. Sayyid Qutb played an important part in guiding Muslim youth along this path, in the latter half of the 20th century, in Egypt in particular and in Arab regions in general ... and he became a model of veracity and an example of perseverance.... The apparently still waters on the surface hid beneath them seething uprisings fomented by the ideas and the call of Sayyid Qutb, and the formation of the contemporary Jihadist cells in Egypt.*

It is undeniable that Wahhabi and Qutbist ideologies lie at the root of numerous murders, assassinations, attacks, massacres, and many civil wars. In the recent past, with the birth of Wahhabism, there have been massacres at Mecca, Medina, and Ta'if, as well as in Jordan, Iraq, Kuwait, and the United Arab Emirates. Even today there are massacres in Algeria, and yet the leaders of organizations which are well-established in the Western world and the Near East openly claim to follow this ideology. They describe Wahhabi ideology and that of Sayyid Qutb as a reformist ideology, and they declare their loyalty to it. They assert that this litera-

---

* Ayman Az-Zawahiri in *as-Sharq al-Awsat*, London, December, 2001.

ture contains "many pages of great beauty." When they talk about massacres, it is never to denounce them vigorously, but to play down their scale. Wahhabites and Qutbists alike justify violence with the promise of Islamic renewal and reform. So the world is full of people who make use of this pretext of Islamic renewal and reformism, in particular Faisal Mawlawi and Fathi Yakan in Lebanon, and Yusuf Al-Qaradawi in Qatar. In France, it is most often the followers of the UOIF, and of Tarek Ramadan, who exploit this theme of reformism.

This so-called "reformism" arouses surprisingly little anxiety or suspicion. For many it is a synonym of progress and modernity. A lot of people actually understand the term reform as an improvement introduced into the moral and social arena. But this is just a sham and it's important to uncover its mechanisms. Herein lie all the symptoms of doublespeak. "Reform" and "reformism," as they are known in France, evoke the 16th-century advent of Protestantism, when *réforme* was advocated in France and elsewhere in the world against the Catholic Church. The Church was suspected of having fossilized both society and religious thinking. The Catholic clergy was accused of every conceivable vice. Protestantism was a phenomenon in Anglo-Saxon countries, and spread a great deal. France, since the Revolution, has been dominated by the concept of *laïcité* (i.e. secularism). So there is a culture, not to say a reflex, by which anyone who appropriates concepts of reform and reformism is elevated. The Qutbists play very insistently on this feeling.

Reformism is appealing for several reasons. Some people like to think they are making an impact, or contributing something to the Muslim world at large. This pseudo-influence takes shape in economic, political, and strategic fields. Others are irked to see Muslims barricade themselves behind their customs and their values. For them the ousting of religion from the public domain represents a step forward. They want Muslim society to set aside traditional religious institutions, in the same way that Europeans have managed to oust the Church. These so-called Muslim reformists lay claim to borrowings from western society's science and modernity.

But the writings of Wahhabi and Qutbist thinkers hold out no such promise. On the contrary, they advocate the destruction of all society and the massacre of populations who obey laws which are not taken from their particular reading of Muslim tradition. Their discourse is all the more distorted because it takes as its target traditional Islam. Qutbists accuse Sunni theologians of preventing their writings from engaging human intelligence, and of of engaging in futile and fossilized factional debates. The goal of this strategy is to do away with what are actually the only bulwarks against extremism and fanaticism within the Muslim community.

Take Sheikh Al-Qaradawi, one of the leading lights of the Wahhabi-Qutbist line of thinking, for example. He has a pretty high media profile as the host of programs on religious topics on Al-Jazeera. According to certain sources, he's also a board member of a bank called At-Taqwa, which has been mentioned in the funding of terrorist organizations. He is featured in UOIF introductory brochures, and was even one of the guests of honor at the organization's 2000 Le Bourget conference in Paris, where he delivered a lecture. What does he write?

Al-Qaradawi criticizes the instruction of points of Islam he deems too technical. In his book *The Worship of God in Islam,*[*] he has this to say: "Let's leave aside the lengthy, hollow and complicated arguments which fill our law books by making distinctions

---

* Yusuf Al-Qaradawi, *L'Adoration de Dieu en islam,* Ar-Risala (1989).

between pillars,* conditions,† obligations, *sunna* (habitual practices), recommendations, revocations and unadvisable matters.... The specialist scholar is permitted to study these terms in this way, provided that it is for himself. But to teach this to ordinary people is, of course, an obvious mistake."

This *fatwa* seeks to denigrate and discredit traditional Muslim instruction. But to replace it with what? With an ideology of terror. Al-Qaradawi defends extremists. In his book *The Tendency to Exaggeration in Excommunication,* he writes, "It is this extremism that has prompted these sincere young people, who are attached to their religion, to excommunicate those opposed to them among Muslims, to kill them and take their goods." But these terrorists have tarnished and distorted the image of Islam in people's minds. How can their criminality, their terrorism and their extremism convey a profound attachment to religion? How dare Al-Qaradawi say that they are "sincere"?

It is easy to see how the pseudo-reformists, with their double-speak, convince the West that they are allies. Let us here interject the tale of the scorpion which, to cross a river, asked a tortoise for a ride on its back. The scorpion repeated to the tortoise that they were allies, with the same interests at heart, and that it would be suicidal for him to harm the tortoise as they crossed the river. The tortoise agreed and took the scorpion on its back, but once in midstream, the scorpion gave the tortoise a fatal sting. And when the dying tortoise asked, "Why did you do that? Now we're both going to die," the scorpion replied, "I can't help it, it's the way I am." So Wahhabis use the West to attack the Muslim world, but the West is also their victim.

---

* Pillars: Rites or demonstrations without which worship is invalid. For example, prostration prior to praying.

† Conditions of validity: Non-rites without which worship is invalid. For example, undertaking minor ablutions before praying.

It is important to lend an ear to Muslims following the instruction of the four traditional Sunni schools: Malikite, Shafiite, Hanafite, and Hanbalite. These Muslims, backed up by arguments and proof, unveil the falsehoods of Wahhabis and Qutbists. To gain an ear within the Muslim community, these latter cultivate the illusion of truth and do their utmost to give the appearance of religious legality. They also use terms which have powerful positive connotations within the Muslim community, for example Muslim Brotherhood and Salafites. Their use of such terms is improper and unjustified, an usurpation with the aim to lead the neophyte astray. This is why it is crucial that the representatives of Sunni Islam wage a determined intellectual struggle. It would be suicidal for our society to sideline those who are the first line of defense against extremism and fanaticism.

4

UPROOTED AND CAST OUT

Our mother painted a negative picture of our family in Morocco, which was so unknown to us. She said that her mother Amina was mean-spirited. She reproached her brother Mouhammad and her sister Zouhour for being too dedicated to bringing up their children. It was as if Zacarias and I didn't have a grandmother, or an uncle, or an aunt, or any cousins. Unlike our sisters, we never saw any of them. Nadia and Jamila would go with my mother on her trips to Morocco. They've got a family. We don't! My mother took Nadia with her because she was proud of her. And she took Jamila along because she was trying to get her married off in the village. One summer she even left her with her brother, so that he could marry her off. But it didn't work.

Sometimes my mother said things which, were they from the mouth of a born-and-bred French person, could be taken as xenophobic. She seemed keen to forget that she was an Arab—she wanted to live the way she chose, without constraints. She made sure that her sons did not have any contact with that world from which she nevertheless had come.

Moroccans are often merry, fervent believers in celebrating Ramadan, the Mawlid, which marks the birth of the Prophet [ﷺ],

or the Eid el-kebir, the celebration of Abraham's sacrifice. But at Roche-Grise, when we were already well into our teens, my mother started to celebrate Christmas. All our North African friends at the vocational school seemed happy to celebrate the Muslim festivals, whereas we hardly knew what they meant. We understood only too well that our family wasn't like any other. Thus a void insidiously formed in us. An abyss which Zacarias and I would both try to negotiate, but in different ways. When we managed momentarily to forget about it, it took just one word bring it back to the surface: "integration."

Throughout our youth this word rang in our ears. At first we didn't understand. We were born here, on this Earth, in this country. We had grown up here. So what did our "integration" mean? How were we to become "integrated" in French society when we were French? Making the shift from childhood to adolescence, and then from adolescence to adulthood, is very upsetting for people who have trouble finding a place for themselves. If, in addition to this identity crisis, you don't have a harmonious family life, then you feel that you belong to nothing. You feel like an unstable electron in a world that is faithless and lawless.

My first recollection of someone hurling a racist remark in our faces goes way back to when we were eight and ten years old. We were living in Mulhouse. At the foot of our apartment block was a large green area, an ideal playground. Every day after school, Zac and I would play marbles with the same friend, a neighbor. One afternoon, at about 4:30, he appeared as usual. We called out to him, "Rémi!" He didn't budge. He looked at us from afar. We walked over to him to ask him what was the matter.

"I can't play with you."

"How come, why can't you play with us?"

"Because my parents said I can't."

"But why have your parents said you can't play with us today? We play marbles together every day."

"No, it's not just today, it's for always. They say that you are niggers, and they don't want me to play with niggers."

Zacarias and I looked at each other, more surprised than hurt. Rémi looked more or less as stunned as we did. He was clearly aware that the words he'd spoken were serious. But he probably didn't really understand them. Nor did we. We were still kids. Even if we intuitively knew what those words meant, we were unable to decipher them. All the more so because we knew very well that we were not "niggers"! That's one of the old memories of racism which keeps haunting me. Little by little we would grow used to it.

At La Fontaine, one of the teachers had a visceral hatred for North Africans. Incredible as it might seem, he did not hide his attitude. When he came across a student of Arab origins in the bathrooms, he would hit him. All the students knew that this went on, but nobody said anything. Zacarias got hit, I got hit, and so did others. In silence. It was *omertà*. As if it only had to do with the teacher and us. As if this was the rule of a game laid on us by a racist teacher. Our goal was to keep one step ahead of him, never to be in the bathrooms when he was there.

In such situations, a child does not really understand what's happening to him. He doesn't know why people are nasty. He simply knows that they are. This is life's apprenticeship. When the child grows up, he learns how not to let it get to him. He learns to use his fists. And when he can lash out, he lashes out. He also learns how to pick out people with prejudices. It's as if a tremendous inner radar system is activated. Unfortunately, it doesn't work all the time—far from it. This is why most young kids in the projects know how to fight. This isn't necessarily the case with young people who live in good neighborhoods.

When we were faced with racism as children, Zacarias and I would go straight to our mother. It was one of the rare things that seemed to get to her. She would be outraged, saying over and over, "They're all racists! They're all racists!" But what could she do? There's something exasperating about displays of ordinary racism. You catch someone in the act, perhaps with witnesses, but there is no outcry. Then you're on your own, left to chew over your bitterness and feel guilty after the fact, for not saying or doing the right thing. But it's already too late, there's nothing to be done. So our mother, for example, couldn't go and confront the supermarket cashier for being rude to us. At best, the cashier would deny it; at worst, she'd create a fuss.

Later on, as young teenagers, Zacarias and I developed a different attitude. The girls we went out with would tell us that their parents disapproved of us and didn't want their daughters hanging out with Arabs. We would just shrug it off. At that age, the way grown-ups saw things didn't matter. We refused to waste our energy thinking about such problems, for which we intuitively knew that we would never find any solutions.

The rise of Le Pen in the political landscape marked a turning point in the history of racism in France. Until the National Front started getting control of town halls, until it chalked up its amazing score in the 1984 European elections, nobody really ever dreamed of admitting to being racist. Certain French people were, but they were ashamed to admit it. Then, when Le Pen started to get so many votes, some stopped hiding their real beliefs. The chorus grew: "France is for the French, we're fed up with immigrants, to hell with wogs, niggers and yids." Louder and louder they claimed "the right to be racist," like it was a wholesome brand of freedom! It was a complete about-face. France would suffer the consequences of it much later on, in the 2002 presidential elections.

Up until that time, there had been little or no idea that so much racism existed, along with a spirit of exclusion. But when certain people around the country started announcing out loud that they loathed foreigners, the fact was that the terms of reference had changed. *Liberté, Egalité, Fraternité* no longer meant anything. We perceived double speak; there was the language of official speeches, and the language of reality. It wasn't a hunch any more, it was a certainty: we were not French "like the others." Or, worse still, we weren't French at all. And yet we were French: we were born in France; we grew up in France; we went to school in France; we spent our childhood and teenage years in France; we had friends in France; and we worked in France.

The years just before you become a teenager are when you start dealing with the bureaucracy on your own—for example, putting together a family dossier for the registrar's office. The form was headed with the words: French citizen. But more often than not, the official behind the window asked Zac and me what our nationality was.

The school cafeteria was also a place of petty, day-to-day snubs. For even if we didn't know anything about religion, still we didn't eat pork. All year round we were obliged to ask the question, "Do you have anything other than pork?" And the whole year long we would get the same response: "Why?"

"Because I'm a Muslim, I don't eat pork."

"Oh for heaven's sake, can't you Muslim people be like everybody else?"

One day a pea and bacon dish was on the menu. When I protested, one of the kitchen staff took my plate, stabbed furiously at the bits of bacon and handed the plate back to me, grumbling, "You're not going to bug us over a few bits of bacon." A classmate who was not a Muslim snapped back at him, "And how would you like it if someone put a few ounces of shit in your plate?" Once again we felt under attack. In fact we were just confused. We couldn't recognize ourselves either in the all-French model, or in the North African model.

Millions of young North Africans and other Africans feel just what Zacarias and I have felt. For children, social life starts at school; what teachers and staff think is incredibly important to them. If children don't feel respected or accepted, they have trouble building a positive image of themselves.

It would take only a little effort on the part of the state school system to make it so that students of Muslim origin would feel a bit less skinned alive. The country must be capable of making this kind of effort. Suffering doesn't help people to think. Pain cannot be intellectualized, it is suffered. And by the time symptoms of the pain start to show in youths, it is already late in the day. Without warning, the aggressiveness and malaise among all these young people can manifest itself in the form of petty delinquency. Or worse...

As kids in Mulhouse, Zacarias and I often said that there really were many racists in France. In Narbonne, the xenophobia was embodied in actual violence. In the summer there were village fairs all over the region. We were seventeen and eighteen by then. Needless to say, these fairs gave us a chance to have some fun and to meet girls. We would happily travel to them, usually hitchhiking. One night, with two other buddies, we went to the Coursan fair, a few miles north of Narbonne. The fair was held in the middle of the town stadium, with several stages and bands. There we met a bunch of young village kids who, it turned out, wanted to beat up some wogs. We left there running for our lives through the vineyards. How many times, when Zacarias and I went to village fairs, did we have to leave like that, running through the vines? For us it was a question of escaping from what were potentially very real threats. Sometimes it was only young kids who'd drunk six or seven beers and just wanted to hit somebody. And sometimes we managed to scare them off—there's often strength in numbers. But there were fights in which fists flew thick and fast.

In Narbonne, on the night of July 14, 1989, an unfortunate thing happened which marked us for good, causing us to feel extremely uneasy, and very suspicious of the powers that be. It was late, getting on to midnight, when I left some Narbonne friends who had asked me to supper. They dropped me off just before it was time for the Bastille Day fireworks in the town square, not far from where my brother and some other friends were waiting for me near the canal. It's a very touristy spot, with lots of bars and outdoor terraces. I had a hundred yards to walk. I was walking quietly along when I felt a tap on the shoulder. I turned around and saw a man who could have been twenty-five or thirty, I don't really know. He said to me, "Please come over here, will you, there's a couple of things I want to say to you. Follow me." I found his behavior weird, so I ignored him and continued walking. I wasn't worried because there were lots of people around.

After ten or fifteen yards, I felt a hand on my shoulder. I turned around, a bit annoyed, but not really bothered, and Pow! The guy landed a punch, full in my face. I fell back into a flower bed. I was completely groggy, but I got up—and saw the guy coming to hit me again. I took to my heels, panicked because I didn't know who he was or why he wanted to hit me. But in my panic I went the wrong way, and ran further from where my brother was waiting. I crossed the street, passed the edge of the square and noticed six or seven cops. I ran straight up to them, shouting, "There's a guy running after me to hit me! Look what he's done!" My face was covered in blood. The cops looked at me suspiciously as I gabbled away. At that moment the guy appeared, went for me, and I dodged him, crying out to the cops, "That's him, that's him!" At that, one of the cops pulled out a tear gas canister. With one hand he grabbed me by the hair and with the other he emptied the tear gas right in my face. I was stunned, my eyes were burning, I was suffocating. I tried to run away, but only managed to go about 100 yards before collapsing in a faint outside a restaurant. Luckily, some friends of mine were eating inside. Because just as they came out to help, the guy appeared again. To finish me off. My friends got in his way and he ran off. They took me to the hospital. My face was burnt by the tear gas. I was in a state of shock, not so much because of the crazy guy, who probably just wanted to "bash a wog," as by the way the cop had behaved. I was the victim, I was asking him for help, and he gassed me.

My mother came to see me at the hospital. She was just as shocked as I was and insisted that I not let this incident go unprotested, that I lodge a complaint against the guy who'd hit me and the cop who'd gassed me. So the following morning I went with my mother to the police station to lodge a complaint. And, would you believe it, we couldn't do anything! Impossible to lodge a complaint. The policeman on duty kept saying, "You know, in the thick of things, it's really impossible to say what's going on." And then, seeing that we were determined, he lost his temper and told us to get out, shouting, "We've got better things to do, just count yourself lucky that it didn't go any further—now clear out!" My mother and I were furious and disgusted.

Later on, a lawyer friend told me that it's possible to lodge a complaint directly with the state prosecutor. I knew some members of an association called *SOS Racisme*, which backed my complaint and made sure it wasn't buried. In the end, there was actually a trial. The guy admitted that he had hit me for no reason. He was given a suspended seven-day prison sentence, and a moderate fine. I never heard if anything happened to the cop.

Zacarias suffered just as much as I did from the incident, if not more. It really enraged us. Can you imagine the frustration of realizing that those who are supposed to protect you in truth pose a threat? The cop didn't just gas and insult me. It was worse than that. For him, quite obviously, it's always the Arab who's guilty. That kind of thing can really fill a person's heart with hatred for a long time.

The hatred faded, but our mistrust remained. Especially in my brother. Later on, with a little thought, I rationalized things. I'm well aware that there's no point in making sweeping conclusions from just one incident. But still today, when I have a problem, my initial reflex is not to go to the cops for help.

Another time, Zacarias went to a disco with his girlfriend. I tried to talk him out of going, because I knew all too well the risks he would face at this club. Every time we went, it ended in humiliation. Just trying to get in was a problem. Most times, we were turned away: "No entry ugly mugs." To avoid such unpleasant scenes, I decided not to go there any more. But Zac was pigheaded. If he wanted to go to a club with Fanny, he went. That night they got in without any trouble; they were a couple, and the bouncer let them through. But inside things weren't so good. Zacarias and Fanny danced a slow number together. A guy tapped my brother's shoulder and punched even before Zac turned around. Blood poured from his mouth. Zacarias lashed back with a head butt and the guy fell to the floor. A second guy came up and Zac broke his collar bone with his elbow. A third guy got involved, and then my brother really got beaten up. And all the time he's being hit, what does he hear? "Had it with these niggers! They're even taking our women!" Throughout the brawl, Fanny was beside Zacarias, sobbing and afraid for him. In the end, the bouncers moved in, took Zac with them and stayed close by him until the club closed. They even went so far as to drive Zac and Fanny home, in case the others were waiting outside to finish him off. Next day, Zac's eyes were swollen and his mouth misshapen. I couldn't help but say, "I told you not to go there!"

One of the three guys who attacked Zacarias went to our school. He was a rugby player. Needless to say, that Monday morning, as Zac's big brother I had to do something. It was only thanks to another student who joined me—spurred on, he would tell me later, by the unequal nature of the fight—that I didn't have my face smashed in turn. The rugby player was twice my size. Two of us only just managed to deal with him. Hatred smoldered between us until the end of the year. In general, the atmosphere was very tough. Some of the students admitted openly to being racists. Actually, they didn't "admit" it so much as boast about it.

Before very long came the difficulty of finding a way into the job market. As young French men of North African origin, we had a sense of deep-seated injustice. We had good grades, but had a hard time finding jobs as trainees. Some bosses were quite frank: "I don't want any Arabs." It goes without saying that there were never any witnesses to this kind of remark. Others reacted in a different way: "I'm very sorry, but we've just taken someone on." Oddly enough, the very next day a classmate would tell you that he got the job you were after. What were you to think? This is one of the really perverse side-effects of racism; there are times when you have doubts about yourself and your analytical abilities. You no longer know whether you didn't get that job because your vocational qualifications were not as good as those of your classmate, or because of your Arab face. The playing field is never level, and you can easily become paranoid.

Zacarias came up against this problem even more than I did because of a certain new class he took, "Automated Mechanical Systems Maintenance." Over a two-year period he had to put in sixteen trainee weeks in firms. Students had to find a firm that would agree to train them. As a rule, they found their placements through acquaintances, by pulling strings, or by luck. Zacarias and all the other students of North African and African origin had to rely for help on a handful of teachers who were well aware of the problem. One teacher, Mr. Dupont, was a wonderful man. Zacarias and I didn't need to explain to him that we were having trouble finding jobs because we were Arabs. He knew how things worked. He didn't tell us that he would help us, either: discretion on the part of victim students, and discretion on the part of a realistic teacher. We knew he understood. It was Mr. Dupont who got Zac recruited as supervisor at the Victor Hugo secondary school, which kept a roof over his head and food on his plate.

Even today, some within the state educational system elect to deny the problem of racism and discrimination. The first time I saw the topic taken head-on by a teacher was when I myself was a supply teacher. In the middle of an electro-technical certificate meeting, a colleague took the floor and said, "How do I manage to find courses for my North African students, when I have bosses who say to me, 'We don't want any Arabs'?" The official answer is straightforward: there are laws in France against racial discrimination. All in all, racism in the workplace is still a reality, but now there are more crackdowns; nowadays, you can speak out about it openly.

5

ZAC'S DREAM: A PLACE IN THE SUN

At the end of the summer of 1986, it was my turn to leave Roche-Grise. I told my mother that I was going to live with Zacarias, that it would be better for my kid brother not to be on his own anymore. At the time she didn't say anything. Zac and I had temporary work as laborers all summer, building roads, cleaning drains under bridges, and the like. It was very physical work and enabled us to put a bit of money aside. I begged my mother to come with me to rent a studio apartment near the main square in Narbonne. Not to pay the deposit, just to show the owner that I was totally committed. To my surprise, she agreed. So Zac and I rented the studio, and found some independence and peace of mind.

Meeting rent was a challenge. We had to find odd jobs. Luckily we could eat in the school cafeteria. Zacarias got his vocational certificate, and decided to get back onto an academic track. It would really be "swimming against the current." For my part, I was in the last year of my electrical engineering degree.

Our dinner diet consisted of pasta and potatoes. Sometimes friends invited us to eat with them—we never refused. We were led by our stomachs: "Let's go and see so-and-so, his fridge is always full." Often we felt more than a bit guilty. But Zacarias refused to consider asking mother for help. Anyway, he had Fanny to attend to his every need. As often as she could, she brought him bags full of food, and lots of vitamin-rich fruit juice. Now and then, when he was in a good mood, he would share with me. Day-to-day living was not easy, and we argued more than before, usually over silly little things.

Winter came. The strikes resulting from university reform proposals presented us an opportunity; we offered our apartment as headquarters of the Student Committee. Enlightened militancy—the fridge was always full. By the end of the school year we were exhausted, both mentally and physically. Zacarias nevertheless moved into the final baccalaureate year, and I obtained my certificate of technical education.

Just before the school year ended, we moved again. A friend's mother agreed to put us up in a fairly large, but rather unhealthy apartment. In exchange, we undertook to do some work on it for her—work, it turned out, that was really beyond us. The walls were covered with mold. The wallpaper was peeling. Our clothes were always damp. Zacarias was often ill; he had a permanent cold and endless throat infections.

The ever-resourceful Fanny brought him medicines. It was out of the question for him to fall seriously ill, because it was his baccalaureate year. Fortunately, that was the year Mr. Dupont pulled strings and got him the assistant supervisor job at Victor Hugo, where he had room and board during the week. So for him at least, only weekends and school holidays were hard.

Although we made no effort to contact our mother, we crossed paths with her now and then; Narbonne is a small city. Zacarias would ignore her, and she him, but I would say hello—after all, she was our mother. I tried to make sure that these meetings didn't last too long. As soon as she had a chance, she would let rip with criticisms of Zacarias. He and I hardly ever talked about it, because the whole topic triggered a silent bitterness in him.

Despite his problems, Zac got his vocational baccalaureate. Then he passed the entrance exams for the technical and commercial advanced vocational diploma in Perpignan, and elected to study mechanical and electrical engineering.

Zacarias's life was finally about to change. He would get a study grant and a room in a dorm. His day-to-day needs would be taken care of, if our mother agreed to hand over the necessary papers to apply for the study grant. An illusory wish. Instead, year after year, Zacarias and I had to line up with a social worker, and then put together dossiers (never with the required formalities) to present to the local education authority. Luckily the application eventually was accepted. It would seem that this kind of situation is very common when parents and grown-up children do not get along.

The following summer we broke up stones and mended roads, as usual. In September, Zacarias went to Perpignan and took a room in the dorm. Fanny was close at hand. She had enrolled in a degree program in advanced sales and marketing, and rented a small apartment in the center of the city. They more or less lived together, using the university room as a pied-à-terre, and for visitors. For my brother this was the beginning of the student's good life. Meanwhile, I was back in Narbonne preparing for the baccalaureate, and working in turn as assistant supervisor at Victor Hugo. So during the week there were forty miles between us. But weekends we usually met up. Zacarias came back regularly from Perpignan. He had also rented a small studio in Narbonne, which he used when Fanny went to see her parents.

Even on weekends when Zacarias's apartment was empty, I stayed in the dorms. Oddly enough, Zacarias never suggested that I use his place. For a while, he seemed to have changed. I felt that we had grown apart. The previous two years had seen some strain in our relationship. We had had some bad arguments. Instead of drawing us closer, hard times had pushed us apart. I was working for the baccalaureate, and I didn't have much time to work things out. Zacarias spent most of his time with Fanny. He had mid-term exams to prepare for, and the other demands of his student life.

I passed my baccalaureate with distinction, and enrolled in turn in the vocational training program at Perpignan. I rented a dorm room. Zac was now living in Fanny's apartment. That academic year, 1989-90, would be a year dedicated to partying. My brother and I were together as university students. Every night we ate with this friend or that. When Zacarias went to Narbonne, he saw Yves, who had been a secondary-school friend. Dave, whom he'd known just as long, was in his class. So he had old friends around him. He also spent time with a Swiss student who was an arms enthusiast.

Every couple of months, we had three days of mid-terms. For those three days we did do some work.

Even though Zacarias was always going out on the town, often without Fanny, he was amazingly faithful to her. This actually made the girls even more attracted to him. They would flirt with him in hopes of landing "a prize catch." No such luck!

At the end of the summer of 1990, driving back from the Paris area, I stopped off in Narbonne to say hello to Jamila. I tooted the horn outside my mother's house. My sister emerged from the basement, where her room was, with another girl. Jamila introduced us. The girl was Fouzia, my aunt's daughter—so my cousin. She had come to France to study as a postgraduate. We talked about our respective studies, and I offered to take her down to Perpignan. There I introduced her to Zacarias, and they immediately got on well. Fouzia told us things about our family that we had never heard before. She drew a picture of a harmonious, fulfilled family. We spent whole evenings asking her about this family member or that. All of a sudden we were much more interested in it all. Fouzia's background was totally different from ours. Her family was close-knit, you could feel how much she loved them all. Her parents took an interest in what was happening with her. They phoned her regularly. She told us that they were paying for all four of their children's higher educations. Naturally enough, Fouzia tried to patch things up between us and our mother. But Zacarias told her how much Aïcha had disappointed him, and warned her about Aïcha's fits.

In no time, Zacarias and I grew very fond of Fouzia. We were proud to have such a cousin. We introduced her to all our friends and they liked her, too. Zacarias, who was so discreet about his life with Fanny, introduced the two. Zacarias and Fouzia talked a great deal about their respective studies and ambitions. He told her about his import-export project between France and North Africa. He also talked with her about what she might study. He advised her about the skills that go the farthest in the job market, and gave her practical tips for her interviews. We helped her with her administrative paperwork. Then she enrolled at Marseilles University, and when the university term came around we went our different ways. In the next year I rarely saw Fouzia, and Zacarias didn't see her at all, although they said hello to each other through me. My brother felt a fraternal and protective love for his cousin.

Zacarias seemed to be leading a stable life. He was living with the girl he loved and got his vocational certificate without too much trouble. He had finally sorted out his financial problems, too. He bought a car, a Ford Fiesta. He was student supervisor at a secondary school in Saint-Pons, west of Montpellier. Incidentally, it was a job he nearly didn't get—the letter from the education authority offering him the job went to Aïcha, and never reached Zac. Luckily, when he told me that they were really late answering him, I advised him to get in touch directly with the education authority.

Fanny also got her diploma in Sales and Marketing. She started studying law. My brother lived with her when he wasn't at the Saint-Pons school, where he slept three nights a week. He enrolled at Montpellier in a degree course in Economic and Social Administration.

As usual, Zacarias was very demanding. His certificate credits didn't transfer fully to the university. He had to make up some credits and he didn't like that. What was more, the university system was much less structured than the advanced vocational certificate, for which students had thirty-five hours of classes a week, and were closely supervised by the teachers. University meant freedom; you had to be self-motivated, because nobody was forced to attend lectures. Beneath his assertive demeanor, Zacarias needed to be guided, supported and reassured by his teachers. But at university teachers have very little to do with their students. Supervised projects are overenrolled, and students have to set up tables in corridors. Zacarias was left to his own devices.

Some of his friends went on to business school, which was unthinkable for him because tuition was too high, forty thousand francs a year. Others found jobs. He, too, vaguely looked for work. But he tended to be very quickly discouraged and suspected that each refusal was racially motivated. He gradually let himself go. He became more and more unmotivated, and seemed to come to view his student days in a negative light. He had no aim or goal. He was gloomy and weary. Zacarias was sure that he had done his very best to get back into an academic curriculum, only to be fettered, at the last minute, by invisible but real chains—the chains of discrimination. Then there was the hard reality that his advanced vocational diploma would not be enough to work as a sales technician.

He told me that at the national employment agency some of the job ads were color-coded. Depending on the color, the job-seeker knew whether the company would accept people of foreign origin or not. He also said that the personnel at the employment agency knew very well where it was useless to send an applicant who was an immigrant. The school year passed as a mix of frustration and questioning. The evenings we spent with our friends were full of laughter, but also discussion: it was the period of the Gulf War.

In our part of France, things had become quite tense. To the point where local politicians started to worry that there might be a violent confrontation between the born-and-bred French population, and citizens of North African origin. For a while, the mayor of Perpignan ordered gun shops closed. In classes, the students quickly split into two factions: the "pro-Americans," who applauded when they saw the bombings in Iraq, chanting, "USA! USA!"; and the "pro-Arabs," those who were touched by the plight of Iraqi civilians under American bombs. The dorm was abuzz with the war in Iraq. The campus was a melting pot, where all kinds of ethnic groups lived together. A scaled-down version of the world. There were Swedes and Danes, as well as Christian Lebanese, Palestinians, and Syrians. And from the very outset of the Gulf War, the dialogue between the Arabs and the others was complicated. No, we did not go along with Saddam Hussein's regime. But we wholeheartedly condemned the Americans and their allies for tossing bombs at civilians. Zacarias wasn't living in the dorm, but we hung out with the same friends on campus and he was very supportive of the Iraqi people. Zacarias with his dark skin, and his girlfriend with her blonde hair and blue eyes—they both knew what xenophobia was.

One evening I was waiting for the bus to go back to the dorm when a guy in a car stopped right beside me. He got out and walked fast toward me, screaming. He was brandishing a knife. "Dirty wog,

I'm going to get you!" he yelled. My reflexes kicked in and it saved my skin. I levelled him. No-one at the bus stop lifted a finger. When I told my brother what had happened, his face turned pale and his lips tightened, and he didn't say a word.

Student debates inevitably gravitated not only to the Gulf War, but also to the situation in Palestine, and the civil war in Algeria. Decisive conflicts for all Muslims throughout the world. For hours we talked about the legitimacy of the intervention in Iraq. For us, Saddam Hussein had no right to invade a country the way he had; but neither was anyone entitled to massacre the Iraqi people in response. We were shocked by the "war show," which was so over-hyped by the media, and in such a one-sided way. The so-called surgical strikes sickened us.

We empathized with those suffering people, not only because they were suffering, but also because they were Muslims. Initially, Saddam Hussein tried to play on the empathy of fellow Muslims. But in no time at all, Arab countries sent in their armies to defend Kuwait. For we Muslims it was a disconcerting war. It wasn't good guys versus bad guys. The truth was more subtle. The war crystallized feelings against American imperialism, political and economic. Zac, myself, and our friends felt that the France that sent in troops to fight alongside the Americans was not our France.

I think it was at that particular moment that Zacarias started to feel that he belonged to the "blacks," whereas people of French extraction were "whites." He became convinced that the French are racists. That generalization didn't scare him. For him, his friends and my friends, and Fanny, too, and the few teachers who had helped us were "non-racist" French. They were exceptions to the rule. I often tried to tone down his ideas. But every day that he witnessed racism confirmed his painful conviction. The fact was, since the outbreak of the Gulf War, attacks against the North African community became more and more frequent, at least in the south of France where we lived.

And then there was the war in Yugoslavia and Bosnia. The media crudely reported the ethnic cleansing and the massacres of Muslims. Feelings in the Muslim community ran deep—Yugoslavia was just an hour and a half from Perpignan. And it was Europe. There were Yugoslavian students on campus. We identified easily with them. Photos of concentration camps with emaciated, sick Muslim prisoners started to circulate: photos all too reminiscent of images from our history books of Jews being shipped off to Nazi concentration camps. The French government seemed to us to be terribly passive, not to say uncooperative. We felt hurt and humiliated. These people were our brothers. The other European countries were not reacting; even the systematic rape of Bosnian women by Serbs didn't seem to ruffle many feathers. Wasn't it true that the governments weren't doing anything because the victims in Bosnia were Muslims? Who can guarantee us that one day the same horror won't be visited upon us French Muslims, and who can guarantee us that other peoples will be any less passive?

Gulf War, Bosnia, Algeria, Palestine, Afghanistan, Chechnya... Muslims were being persecuted all over the world. That disgusted us. Zacarias wasn't the only one who felt wronged. All Muslims our age, and even those who were younger, were shattered. They felt deeply and personally, in their very flesh, the injustices visited on their religious brothers. As they grew older these young Muslims became hypersensitive. They no longer believed in the morality and ethics of rulers. Some of them grew ripe for the indoctrination of totalitarian and sectarian ideologies. I was assailed more often than my brother by brutal racism, yet he suffered more than I did. Every attack on his older brother put him in uncontrollable states of inner torment.

When I told him he was wrong, that whatever he might think, the majority of French people were not racists, I did not merely fail to convince him. The only ear he lent me was an irritated one. He would inevitably answer, "Abd Samad, you're too nice. You haven't realized that they're all racists and fascists."

In September, 1991, Zacarias needed an administrative certificate from the university to keep his job as supervisor at the secondary school. Buoyed by his new plan to speak fluent English, he enrolled in the Applied Foreign Languages course at Perpignan. But he would hardly ever set foot in a class there—instead, he got a new job as a supervisor in the Docteur La Croix secondary school in Narbonne. I also found a job as a supervisor in Narbonne, at the Diderot secondary school.

When that term started we met Fouzia again. She had had a good university year, and embarked on her degree in pharmacology. During her stay at Roche-Grise, Fouzia had witnessed our family disputes. She was truly shocked and her relations with my mother deteriorated a lot. Zacarias and I advised her to keep her distance. Finally the break was made; Fouzia left Roche-Grise with the words, "I don't understand this situation, it's too much for me, I've finished my studies, and my resident's permit expires soon, so I'm going back to Morocco." Zacarias and I approved of her decision. But she was not departing immediately, and we had to find her somewhere to stay in the interim. Zacarias and I both lived at the schools where we worked. So I asked my sister Nadia, who had an apartment in the middle of Narbonne, to put up our cousin for ten days. She agreed. Zacarias, Fouzia, and I spent those days together. As soon as work was over, we met up. We went for walks and saw our friends. I still have a few distinct memories of those days, like the film we saw one Wednesday afternoon. We'd forgotten that it was children's day, so the three of us ended up with just a handful of other grownups in a cinema full of kids. Remembering the incongruousness of that particular moment brings back the good feelings between us. We went to Perpignan, too, to stay with friends. One of my closest friends was called Xavier. We spent our evenings talking and laughing and would always end with a really nice meal. The day before Fouzia left, we met my two sisters, and all five of us went for a walk. We spent that evening with Nadia, over a meal. At the end of October, 1991, Zacarias and I went with Fouzia to Sète, where she would take the boat *Marrakech*. We laughed a lot on the journey. Those were rare moments of family happiness. It had been a long time since we siblings had been together.

Talking about our family with Fouzia had aroused in Zacarias and me a desire to know more about our father. We wanted to know what had become of him. The latest we'd heard, he was in Toulouse, so after we left Fouzia in Sète, we drove to the pink-brick city. Once there, we got into detective mode. Thanks to the Chamber of Commerce and Local Industry, we got an address, only to find that he was no longer living there. Then Zacarias and I had the bright idea of contacting the customer service department of the Electricity Company, with one of us pretending to be our father. We complained that we hadn't had the latest bill, and told the employee that there was a problem of addresses, and we wanted to check to see if the one on file was the right one. Bingo! She gave us our father's address, and thanks to her we found him. He was very moved by our visit. We spent a warm evening with him. Naturally enough, he invited us stay the night. At dawn we were awakened by fearful noise and shouting: "Police! Police! Open up!" We hardly had time to pull back the covers before five or six cops were in the apartment. They took our father away while we looked on dumbfounded. Everything happened so fast. Then the apartment was empty. A deathly silence crept in. We got dressed and set off back to

Narbonne. We hardly spoke during the drive, both lost in our thoughts. Why exactly had the police taken him away? Only ten years later did I learn the reason—it involved some kind of brawl.

I think that was the last time Zacarias saw our father. I bumped into him again in 1993, in Narbonne, as I left school at the end of the week. I was with my sister Nadia at the railway station. He didn't look well; he'd lost a lot of weight and seemed tired.

Zac and I had become very close again. We were once more living in the same city. We both worked as supervisors, we shared the same friends, and spent evenings together. When Zacarias talked to me about his work, he was critical of the administrative staff. Once again, he found them aggressive and stupidly racist. He claimed, for example, that all the supervisors of foreign origin had to work the worst hours. For him, racism had become an obsession. Whether founded or no, his obsession was now wrecking his life.

For Zacarias and Fanny, as a couple, things were getting more complicated. It now seemed crucial to Zac to add something extra to his training, which would make the difference in the eyes of a potential employer. We talked about it every weekend. As we had a female cousin in the United Arab Emirates, we started imagining how our life would be if one day we did business in Arab countries, and particularly Morocco and the Emirates. Zacarias found out about a Montpellier-based association called Euro-Arabe, which dealt trade between North Africa and Europe.

Zac thought that the wisest thing, first of all, would be to improve our language skills. At the time he spoke just broken English, and no Arabic, so he bought text books and worked away at English grammar. Every day he forced himself to study in the most serious way you could imagine. After a few months, my brother realized that he hadn't chosen the best way to go about it; he still hadn't achieved any kind of fluency. As we talked it over, we eventually agreed that there was nothing like real experience in an English-speaking country. He thought he might find a job as supervisor on the spot, as in France. If he was eligible for a state-funded loan, he would look for an appropriate course. Later on he would have a chance to learn Arabic, and thus be able to work as a sales technician in export between French-speaking countries, English-speaking countries, and the Emirates.

In Montpellier, Zacarias hung out at the dorm cafeteria. It was an odd kind of place. The students who spent half their day there were mostly foreigners—Moroccans, Algerians, Tunisians, Malians, Senegalese, Syrians and Palestinians. Many of them used the cafeteria like a squat, because they had accommodation problems, especially those in their last two years, when as a rule they were given a room only once everyone else had been housed. So they would end up five or six to a room, and sleep there in rotation. If it wasn't your turn you had to stay awake, and by day you would be too tired to attend classes. On holidays, the communal kitchens were closed, which made the squatters feel more out on a limb. They all told us about how degrading it was, about the uphill battle they were forced to fight just to be able to study. For example, the administrative departments at the prefecture required a resident's permit in order to issue a student card. And the educational departments required a student card for enrollment. This administrative game-playing went on for months, and students would emerge disgusted and exhausted by the harassment. Most of them ended up saying it would have been better to go and study in the United States or Canada, rather than France.

Added to this precarious immigrant student's life were money problems. The scholarships from their home countries were derisory, and their temporary resident's permit bore a stamp: "Not authorized to work." The most determined and stubborn of them managed nevertheless to attend second-degree courses and embark on doctorates. These students had few class hours, and they looked for odd jobs to help them make ends meet. Some of those who didn't succeed seemed cynical, at a dead end. They spent their time talking about the latest international news. Little by little, Zacarias spent hardly any time with born-and-bred French people. His new friends cultivated an attitude of rebellion. They were forever denigrating politicians and intellectuals, and French ones in particular, railing against their blinkered, single-minded thinking. There were probably Muslim Brotherhood members among them. At the university they had a nickname, "Kid Brothers."

I was particularly shocked by one of them, a North African. He said he'd received a large grant from his home country, yet he spoke like a disenfranchised radical, advocating extreme violence. What bothered me was that he had been helped by a developing country to pursue his studies, from baccalaureate to Ph.D., and instead of contributing to the development of his country, he claimed that it was more important to foment revolution there, in order to destroy society. One of his sentences still rings in my ears: "We have to destroy this society so that it can be born again from its ashes." His source was Sayyid Qutb, whom he described as a "reforming martyr of Islam."

I think I can say without fear of contradiction that it was by rubbing shoulders with these students that Zacarias discovered a dangerous caricature of Islam. Everything that they said was marked by a desire for vengeance. What they had to say about the civil war in Algeria, for example, was extremely dubious. "We don't know what's going on over there. The authorities say it's the Armed Islamic Group (GIA) that is massacring the population, but they don't provide any proof and it's very likely that they are trying to cover things up." This was the same rhetoric peddled by certain leaders of the Islamic Salvation Front (FIS). The students also seemed to use certain tragedies, like war, to their own ends. Whether in Palestine, Bosnia, or elsewhere. For them, every conflict involving Muslims offered a chance to uphold the highly militant argument of the Muslim Brotherhood. The causes were probably just, but here they were conducted by extremist indoctrination, for political and financial ends that would benefit others, not the student practitioners.

The more the university year advanced, the less Zacarias turned up for class. When he returned to Montpellier, he hung aimlessly about on campus, spending more and more time talking with the "Kid Brothers." He, too, started to develop a specific style of argumentation, and his disillusionment and cynicism increased. When it came to Algeria, he would now say that the political elite was really responsible for the civil war and the massacres. When it came to France, he would argue that the system was rotten and made solely to serve a corrupt middle class. He would say that for ordinary, humble people, the only solution was to fend for yourself. I didn't share Zacarias' ideas. I found them excessive, telling myself that it was a difficult year for him, because he felt he was failing and he didn't really see how to make things better. He would often repeat, pessimistically, "I studied so that I could manage better, and what's the result? I'm stuck." Deep down, I thought that the bitterness in him would pass when he finally found his way.

Not having a family home where you can recharge your batteries doesn't help matters. Since leaving our mother's house, Zacarias hadn't set foot in it again. We spent our holidays in the dorm lobbies. When anyone asked him about our mother, Zacarias would inevitably answer, "She's not my mother, she's my brother's mother." The only thing he wanted to do was to leave Narbonne. At every opportunity he would say, "All I know is that I've got to leave. I don't know where to, and I don't know when, but I must leave this city." We talked more and more about the advantages of learning

English. We even drew up ambitious plans. He would speak English fluently; he would learn literary Arabic, the Arabic of the Gulf States. While he learned Arabic, I would learn English in turn. Then we would go into international business together. When his dreams focused once and for all on England (the United States was too expensive and too far away in case things went wrong), I encouraged him to go there. It seemed to me that it was a good opportunity for him to change environments and company. Naively, I reckoned that he would get away from the "Kid Brothers." I knew my brother, and I knew that he was not easily influenced—but you never know.

Fanny wasn't at all in agreement with Zacarias's plan. She had just been taken on as a sales assistant in a bank, and all she dreamed about was having a quiet life, living with Zacarias somewhere nearby. She wasn't at all keen for him to go away. She encouraged him to go on looking for work. Zac blamed her for not being realistic, and not understanding that the color of his skin was a real drawback when it came to finding a job. He also reproached her, "Do you think it'll be easy for us to find somewhere to live, with my skin color? You know very well how things are, don't you? I'd have to be a millionaire to get any respect." These accumulated frustrations were like so much fertilizer for the ideologies that Zacarias unfortunately would encounter in England.

At the end of 1991, everything began to move very fast. Zac sold his Ford Fiesta. He set aside money saved on rent since Fanny and he had left their apartment in Montpellier, and he was very careful about how much he spent. Since his room and board was provided for by the school, he did manage to put a little away, between twenty thousand and twenty-five thousand francs. Together we went to buy a large backpack for his trip. As a safety measure, we bought him a money belt, too. Zacarias set off with all his worldly wealth on his person. He had no idea what he would find where he was going. If somebody robbed him, it would bring his trip to an immeadiate halt. His intention was to stay at least six months in England. Together we bought most of the things he needed. His adventure was a bit mine, too; for the first time he and I were going to be truly parted. He was my little brother. I was at once proud of him, sad, and anxious. I was the only person who went to the airport with him. It was a very solemn moment. My brother was setting off on a rendezvous with his destiny...

6

DOWN AND OUT AND ALONE IN LONDON

Nobody was there to greet Zacarias in London. When he arrived, his first task was to find a place to stay. Before he left, he had reckoned he would easily find a quiet and simple youth hostel. But when he phoned me a few days later, he told me that he'd ended up in St. Mark's House—a homeless shelter. He gave me a phone number where I could reach him, said that everything was fine and that I shouldn't worry; whatever happened, he would make do. He wanted to get in touch with the social services and find ways of getting state benefits. Most importantly he wanted to find work fast. I phoned him regularly, but our conversations were brief. I only really learned any details about his day-to-day life when he came back to Montpellier more than six months later.

When he landed at Frejorgues Airport in Montpellier, I saw right away that my young brother had changed. He had lost weight and he had grown up. But he had a smile on his face and he seemed very happy to see me again. Then he revealed a little pride: he'd managed to last over there for more than six months. As he admitted to me not long after, for the first three months his poor English had literally paralyzed him. He had spent all that time unable to speak, feeling so ill at ease he hardly opened his mouth. He said he felt as if he was physically weakened, plunged into a scary loneliness.

He lived in a rather disreputable place. He described his roommates to me, with a hollow laugh. One of them behaved completely irrationally, taking dozens of different colored pills every day. Another spent the day drinking beer, sprawled on a sofa in the lobby. He was drunk morning to night. Sometimes, when the person running the hostel threw him out, he stayed slumped on the steps of the church, right next door. There was a shared dormitory, with several dozen homeless guys, mainly English, sleeping there every night. Zacarias had an iron bed and kept his clothes rolled in a bundle under his pillow—everything was up for grabs in that place. By day, needless to say, there was no question of leaving behind your belongings. Thievery and violence were everywhere. Zacarias and I talked at great length about all that underlying insecurity. He was tense and anxious, in an almost palpable way. And then I had an idea. You were less likely to be assaulted if you were physically imposing. So I suggested that Zacarias do some bodybuilding. He liked the idea, even though it represented a real financial investment. As soon as he returned to London, two weeks later, Zacarias joined a bodybuilding club. Now and then he found odd jobs, washing dishes in a pizzeria, warehouse man, and the like. Just enough not to fritter away his meager savings entirely.

After those very difficult beginnings, Zacarias started to feel a bit more at ease in London. He had had months to explore the streets. He finally knew how to get around in that huge city. Every day he forced himself to work on his English, alone with his books in a library. Each week he visited an employment agency. He wasn't looking for a job, so much as professional training. He told me that, after taking a whole battery of tests, he managed to get into South Bank University's Master of International Business program. He speculated that the university was a branch of Cambridge University, and that would look good on his future resumé. My young brother still hadn't lost sight of his goal. He still had a mind to get involved with the import and export of *halal* meat—meat slaughtered in accordance with Muslim ritual—with North African countries, for example.

Every time Zacarias came back to France, I felt and saw him becoming harder. He didn't like British society at all. He described to me a country that was gray, rainy and closed. He said that all ethnic communities were tolerated, but the groups didn't mix. They turned in on themselves, living in separate neighborhoods surrounded by invisible barriers. He accused the English of being tolerant only on the surface. "After all this time," he said, "I've met plenty of people of different nationalities. The only ones I don't know at all are the English." Even at the university, contact with English students was superficial. He said he'd met more British students on the Perpignan and Montpellier campuses.

Zacarias had experienced a real psychological shock. The contrast was sharp: previously he had lived with Fanny, his friends and his brother, in his own country; now he was an immigrant in Britain, on his own, unable to speak the language. He rightly saw himself as having fulfilled a personal challenge by standing his ground. That victory gave him more confidence in himself and somehow gave him more gravitas, which would attract Xavier and another friend, Hartium to him. Luckily for Zac he managed to move out of the homeless shelter. He told me that he had received a study grant, the equivalent of 150,000 francs, to pay for a year's tuition plus lodging—a fully furnished, two-room flat in the middle of London. Only later did I learn that the address he gave me was in one of the more elegant parts of town, Nevern Square, in Earl's Court.

Even today, I can't be sure if he really lived in that famous university flat that he described to me, or whether he actually lived in a flat that was as luxurious as the neighborhood. He certainly couldn't have afforded the rent on his own, anyway. Zacarias told me about one of his favorite parts of London, a neighborhood frequented by foreigners, mainly Algerians and Moroccans. When we talked about the civil war in Algeria, we didn't have the same opinions. I knew through the media that members of the Islamic Salvation Front and the Armed Islamic Groups were based in London, and that they were at liberty to express their hatred in the streets and in mosques. I also knew perfectly well that my brother had no religious background. So I decided it was time to send him an explanatory pamphlet about Wahhabism, published by the At-Tawba Mosque in Montpellier. I would realize later that that was a mistake.

Through 1993 and 1994, Zacarias came back to France every four months or so, mainly to see Fanny. Meanwhile, I met my future father-in-law and asked him for Fouzia's hand in marriage. It was a small but very happy wedding. We showed Zacarias the photos. He congratulated us, but said that he was sorry we hadn't told him. He would have come over for it. Knowing his financial situation, that was precisely what we had wanted to avoid.

Every time Zacarias returned to France, he stayed with us. He never talked to us about religion. Yet it was at that time that I myself started to practice Islam. He could have shown a dash of curiosity, but he didn't. On the contrary, he treated my religious practice somewhat mockingly. As a novice, not reading Arabic, I had to write prayers out in large letters on a sheet of paper. Sometime in 1994, I suggested that Zacarias come with me to Friday prayers at the mosque. He refused, preferring to go into town. Today, I see his refusals in a new light. He probably hadn't yet met the people who would become his gurus. Or at least he hadn't yet been truly recruited.

On another occasion, I tried to find a way of entertaining him. It so happened that the mosque was holding an end-of-school-year party. To honor and reward the children, the Association of Islamic Welfare Projects in France (APBIF) organized the party every year. The children put on cultural shows and recited history. One distinctive feature was the singing group. A dozen children sang Arab-Andalusian Sufi chants. They were a roaring success.

Zacarias came with me as far as the entrance to the hall, but refused to go in. He told me it didn't interest him, that it was all just "innovation."* He said he was interested only in the Koran and the *Sunna*.† Just then the imam arrived to preside over the party, and I took the opportunity to introduce my brother to him. A discussion ensued. I asked the imam to tell my brother how one learns the science of religion. Zacarias cut me off, snapping, "Personally, all I need is the Koran and the Sunna to learn about religion. I'm quite capable of getting ahold of books and studying them on my own." The imam replied, "If you are prepared to spend ten years finding out how to do your minor ablutions in the Sunna or the Koran, good luck!"

A strange discussion: Can you become a doctor by learning medicine all on your own, without any teachers, just from books? Who would go and be operated on by someone who claims to have learned about surgery on their own in libraries? On almost all of his visits, Zacarias borrowed my car to go to Narbonne and see Jamila. While she was still living with my mother, they made sure that Zacarias

---

* Innovation or *bidah:* a new act, i.e., one that the Prophet [☮] hadn't practiced or spoken about. There are two categories of *bidah.* The first involves innovations of uprightness. These are in compliance with the Koran, the *Sunna,* unanimity, scholars and the tradition of companions, for example the celebration of the birth of the Prophet [☮]. The second category concerns errors and follies which contradict the Koran, the *Sunna,* unanimity, scholars and the tradition of companions.

† *Sunna:* beliefs and laws revealed to the Prophet Muhammad [☮].

never met with Aïcha. When he arrived at the house, he would honk the horn from a distance, and Jamila would come straight out.

Meanwhile, things were getting difficult with Fanny. The last time I saw them together was in 1993 in Montpellier; they were spending the weekend in a cottage they had rented. Fanny was still working at the bank. She wanted to make a home with my brother. She wanted to have a family and a normal life. She probably asked him to come back to France, but Zacarias's goal was to get rich. "I must keep moving on and earn money," he would often repeat. He refused to give up the possibility of a better future just to please Fanny.

He, in turn, asked her to go to England. But Fanny knew that life was hard over there. What would be the point of her following him, just to have a tough time? They were both at a dead end, and so was their love for each other which had endured for ten years. Zacarias was deeply wounded by her refusal to follow him. Out of respect he had never talked about her to me, but he told me then, "She's a middle-class girl. All she thinks about is her creature comforts and herself. She doesn't really love me." There was a tone of scorn and pain in his voice. He was terribly disappointed. That marked the end of their love affair. Zacarias is very sentimental, all or nothing. His disillusionment was on par with his passion. He would have moved mountains for Fanny. He felt she wasn't ready. But was it really necessary to move mountains?

When Zacarias came back the following year, I found him quite different. Usually, whenever we were reunited, we talked freely and warmly. As brothers do who have shared memories, moments of great happiness and moments of real pain, from the word go. But this time I suddenly realized how powerless I was. I was simply unable to engage him in any conversation. My brother was there right next to me, and yet I felt he was far, far away. As if he wasn't there at all. He answered my questions about his daily life perfunctorily. Fouzia and I thought that maybe he needed some privacy, to be alone, but would-n't dare say so. So we let him stay in our little apartment, on his own, and we stayed in my office at the school. Zacarias also had use of our car and we left the refrigerator filled for him.

In the evenings my wife would prepare tasty little dishes for him. Fouzia is a great cook. However, not only did this not cheer him up, but he complained. Fouzia was taken aback by this change in his attitude toward her. Up until then, he'd always shown great affec-tion for her, he had always been courteous and attentive. At the end of 1992, on his first trip back from England, the three of us had had great times laughing and dreaming about the future. Up until 1994, Zacarias and Fouzia had always had deep conversations. They talked about their respective studies, and job prospects. Fouzia was work-ing toward her teaching certificate in biology, and Zacarias would encourage her to work even harder, saying that because she was gift-ed she ought to take her studies as far as she possibly could. But now his tack had radically altered. He no longer seemed in favor of studying, at least not for women. He would say over and over to Fouzia, "Studies aren't important for women. You'd be better off staying at home, in your house."

One night when the three of us were watching a film on TV in which a woman was hit by her husband, Zacarias said, "Serves her right, that's what women need." Fouzia and I were aghast. My brother, an undeniably intelligent young man, who was usually open, ready to talk about things, and interested in other people, was more and more becoming an introvert. When he did say something, it was to make aggressive remarks or to promote reactionary ideas. He could spend a whole day without talking, and he never went out of the house. He stayed slumped in an armchair, and if you went on at him and asked him questions, he would answer with a simple "Yes," or just a "No." Needless to say, his behavior worried me. I thought that he had lost his bearings and that a serious depression was imminent. I asked him, "Are you sure things are okay? Can I do something for you? Anyway, you know you can count on me." But he would mechnically reply, "No, it's nothing, I'm tired. You know I've been having a hard time for months...." I tried to get him to change his ideas. To show him that he was important to me, that I loved him, that he was my younger brother and that he could rely on my help. My wife and I tried to reassure him. But I felt helpless. He'd become a stranger.

The year was 1995. Zacarias went back to London to get his Master of International Business (MIB) degree—or so he said.

The next time I saw him was in a photo, a few days after September 11, 2001.

In Montpellier, a few weeks after those tragic events, I met a teacher friend, a born-and-bred Frenchman who had converted to Islam and had been living in Great Britain for the past fifteen years. He was very informed about extremist movements. When we met we had an illuminating discussion about the situation in Great Britain. In his opinion, although the great majority of Muslims in England are Sunnis and essentially Hanafites, the country is rife with sects and extremist organizations. Until September 11, 2001, the British government hardly seemed bothered; it was only when serious incidents occurred, like the attack in Yemen organized by Abu Hamza, that it seemed to take notice. After the Yemen attack the allowances payable to Omar Bakri—former director of *Hizb ut-Tahrir* (the Party of Liberation), and founder of the *Jama'at Al-Muhajirun* (the Immigrants' Movement)—were suddenly and decisively cut off, because Parliament found it scandalous that a man openly preaching the destruction of the British state could be the beneficiary of institutional financial support. My friend told me that Wahhabi movements in England are part of a whole host of diverse organizations, usually inimical to one another, essentially devoted to recruiting members from the Muslim youth of the country. Until September 11, the rule that these extremists seemed to abide by was "no attacks in Great Britain," as long as they enjoyed a completely free hand within the Muslim and the Caribbean communities there.

In one small Muslim neighborhood in London, there is a large mosque run by a Wahhabi movement from the Indian subcontinent called the *Ahl-e Hadith* (the people of the *hadith*).* It also runs a bookshop, a prayer center, a primary school, and a training school for adults belonging to another Wahhabi movement—the so-called Salafites, who are officially in line with the doctrine of the Saudi State. My friend told me how *Ahl-e Hadith* apparently benefits from huge financial backing; its small membership could not alone support so many facilities, or recruit so many people from the Caribbean.

The distinctive feature of the Wahhabi movement is plentiful funds. Also notable is a brutal and contemptuous attitude toward the local Muslim population. Wahhabi groups do not support the present Saudi government, even though their religious authorities (Ahmad ibn Taymiyya [1268–1328], Ibn Al-Qayyim Al-Jawziyya [1292–1350], Muhammad ibn Abd al-Wahhab [1703–1792], etc.) are the same as those of the so-called Salafites and other *Ahl-e Hadith*-like groups. My teacher friend told me that the "Salafites officially declare themselves to be against all forms of terrorism and distribute a pamphlet written by one of their current leaders, Ibn Baz, denouncing the attacks in Saudi Arabia organized by bin Laden. Their politics seem to be in keeping with those of the Saudi Ministry of Religious Affairs."

---

* *Hadith,* or prophetic tradition: a word, fact, or event recounted by the Prophet [ﷺ] or his companions.

In any event, these brother enemies, the Wahhabis and the Saudis, teach their members that they are the only believers on earth, and that other Muslims are a bunch of superstitious and idolatrous ignoramuses. They are notorious for their intolerance of non-members, and their verbal and physical abuse of anybody who stands up to them is well-known. My friend had first-hand experience of it. He said the Wahhabis have a very powerful presence, not only among students preparing for their A-levels (aged sixteen to eighteen), but also in universities. Wahhabis set up so-called Islamic Societies, and Koran and Sunna Societies, which organize activities and courses, and give general assistance to those in need. Or they work their way into existing societies, gain control, and turn them into a branch of their movement within the establishment. Their preachers, and theirs only, come to indoctrinate young audiences who are uninformed and frustrated by the pitiful state of their local and international community. These brainwashing sessions are called "lectures," or talks. According to my friend, to wrest control of a student association from this movement, you have to fight tooth-and-nail against an administration which has no idea about what is going on, and which has its own reasons for turning a blind eye. A student or a young foreigner who goes to England, or a young person with immigrant parents, will make contact with a markedly Sunni community, in which most of the teachers and religious dignitaries speak only Urdu, Arabic, or Bengali. In fact the only religious literature in English that you find in any quantity is Wahhabi. Wahhabis have lots of bookshops. They hand out large numbers of pamphlets and booklets in the street and in markets, and even in the main shopping streets in city centers.

My learned friend sees a real generation gap within the Muslim community in England. On the one hand are parents and grandparents who are too ignorant to quench young people's thirst for knowledge, and religious people who do not really have the powers of expression to communicate effectively with them; and on the other hand is a host of young preachers and writers, with a very solid foothold in colleges and universities, who can speak to curious youth but are out of touch with religious tradition. "One day," my friend told me, "one of my students, talking about the young people arrested in Yemen after being sent there by Abu Hamza, told me that he reckoned he'd had a narrow escape, because he and his friends were well on the way to becoming future Abu Hamza volunteers. In the end, because they started to learn about religion with a Sunni teacher, they moved away from that group and thus got out of the grips of that harmful influence."

This friend gave me three examples of the sort of thing that went on, on a regular basis, in the Muslim community in London up until September 11. First, he went to a lecture at an Islamic association given by a recruiting agent from one of the organizations training people in Afghanistan. This association often invited all kinds of people to hear their ideas, sometimes even non-Muslims—such as people in the hierarchy of the Catholic church. A young man lectured to an audience of about a dozen young people, all in their twenties. He spoke with deference for Sheik Omar Abdar-Rahman, who was imprisoned by the Americans in the wake of the 1993 attack on the World Trade Center. He made much of the humiliating and degrading treatment to which the authorities had subjected Omar. He then recited a litany of war facts, repeatedly invoking the victories of the Afghan resistance during the Russian occupation. Little by little he worked the young people into a state of great agitation. By the end, my friend saw plainly that one or two in the audience were ready to follow this guy. The speaker boasted about the power of his organization (though my friend didn't recall him mentioning the name) and the fact that nobody seemed able to touch them.

Second is the case of a man who calls himself "Sheik" Abdullah Faisal, who was arrested shortly after September 11 as a result of emergency measures taken by the British government. Prior to that Faisal, who is of Jamaican extraction, had studied at Riyad University in Saudi Arabia, and had travelled the length and breadth of England preaching *jihad* with great vigor. He was well-known for his extremely uncompromising attitude. Although he had never fought in the *jihad* himself, his message everywhere was that everyone should head for the front, and anyone who didn't was a heathen. My friend told me that when a young woman said to Faisal that her husband did not wish to leave, and preferred to wage the *jihad* by teaching Islam, Faisal told her that her husband had become an apostate and that as a result their marriage was null and void. The young woman left her husband after hearing this. A former follower of this Faisal left him because he was bored by his continual excommunications. He thought he was the only Muslim on earth; anybody who disagreed with him over the tiniest little thing was treated like a heretic.

The third example was related to my teacher friend by a Muslim colleague. The colleague complained about one of his cousins, who was causing trouble among their relatives. His cousin had gone to the center of the so-called Salafites, who managed to recruit him. Seeing that his bonds with his family might get in the way, they told him not to worry about his wife. Anyone not following them was an idolater, whose marriage with one of their members had no validity. They were prepared to provide him with a wife. (Their women are easy to identify because usually they are clad in a *burqa*—a long, black cloak covering from head to foot—and they also wear a veil, and usually black gloves.) Back home, the young man started to lay into the Sunni beliefs and traditions of his family. When his family became worried over the consequences for his marriage, he told them that his new friends had promised to find him another wife. This teacher was truly shocked—his cousin's family was totally distraught and at a loss.

It is well-known that when a family member falls under the influence of Wahhabis, the recruit's fanaticism causes his relatives colossal problems, because Wahhabis don't accept any half-measures. You're either totally with them or totally against them. From what my friend managed to gather, most of the young people who fall into the clutches of Wahhabi sects end up leaving them either sickened or exhausted. After all, it's not easy to belong to a small group which is hated and feared by the community, which hardly lets you have any private life, and keeps tabs on every little thing you say. Even for a dropout the scars live on. Much of the damage done is irreparable. In the meantime, during his period with these extremists, the recruit is ready to do quite literally anything.

Another problem with Wahhabi recruits is their attitude toward women, and relations between the sexes. My friend has told me that, according to a woman teaching Islamic studies at a college, two young Wahhabis demanded that she hold two separate lessons, one for the boys, and another for the girls. She sent them packing, but often faces similar problems. Another female colleague, who ventured into a Wahhabi bookshop to look for a book for class, told my friend that she was shocked at how fiercely the shopkeepers had tried to ignore her, and with what ill will they'd ended up serving her. I don't know if she realizes that we other Muslims have to live all the time with these people, as neighbors or as relatives.

By way of conclusion my teacher friend said that little of consequence has changed since September 11. Life for Muslims has become much trickier because of the open hostility shown by non-Muslims after the attacks on the World Trade Center. Only those extremists who overtly preached violence and had obvious links with Al-Qaeda are hassled. As for all the Wahhabi groups who officially reject terrorism, they are still everywhere in our community, enjoying impunity, with funding that seems bottomless. Meanwhile, Sunni Muslims have to travel the country, going from mosque to mosque, just to scrape together enough money to build a neighborhood mosque. If they're in a hurry, then they have to turn to Saudi Arabia for funding, which is easily had, but at a price— Wahhabi preachers and books included.

The attitude of the British authorities and organizations (police, educators, etc.) toward Wahhabis is exactly the same as that of the British Government with regard to Saudi Arabia. In private, they acknowledge that they are backward, misogynistic and fanatical. But officially they defend them, claim that they are not in a position to meddle in their affairs. They turn a blind eye to their excesses, heave a sigh and carry on as ever. They know that the terrorists' ideology is exactly the same as the ideology of the so-called Salafites and their kin; they know too that their differences actually have to do with their allegiance to the Saudi religious authorities and government (two problems that are at once separate and connected). Meanwhile, for most young people coming from an immigrant background, and for converts and foreign students, the first message to come to them in their own language, through the most modern media (the Internet is full of Wahabbi sites), and by way of a whole host of preachers, lecturers, and writers, is the message of Wahhabism and other extremist groups.

I find the lack of consideration toward women on the part of Wahhabi followers extremely shocking and scandalous. But when you become acquainted with the concepts and claimed *fatwas* spread about by their leaders, you get a better idea of the roots of this scourge. Here is an example. With regard to women working, the Kuwaiti newspaper *Al-Qabas* published a fatwa by Ibn Baz, former Mufti of Saudi Arabia:

...the call for women to go forth and take part in areas which have to do with men is a very serious act for Muslim society. One of the major effects of this is the mixing of sexes which is regarded as one of the greatest forms of fornication which massacre society and destroy its values.*

Another Wahhabi leader, Al Uthaymeen, observes on the matter of women driving cars:

Of course the driving of cars by women encompasses many misdeeds. Among these misdeeds, the fact that the woman driving must uncover her face. Now, the face is an element of attraction which is particularly sought after by men's eyes. In fact a woman is only considered beautiful or ugly in an absolute sense on the basis of her face. In other words, when one says of a woman that she is beautiful or ugly, the mind thinks only of the face, but when one focuses on other elements one then says that she has beautiful hands, beautiful hair, beautiful feet. So it is indeed the face which is the focus when one attributes beauty to a person. Some people may say that it is possible for a woman to drive without unveiling her face. She could veil the lower part of her face and wear dark glasses. The answer to this is that it is contrary to the customs of women to drive cars. Ask those who have observed them in other countries. Even if we admit that it is possible to apply this solution at the outset, it will not last very long, but will swiftly evolve towards the same situation for women as in other countries.

---

* *Al-Qabas,* Friday 14 June 1996

This is a good example of the regressive evolution Wahhabis foster. The argument, to start with, appears more or less acceptable, but there is then a downward spiral toward rejected and unacceptable viewpoints.

> Among the offenses intrinsic to the driving of cars by women, there is the disappearance of propriety... Because those who drive cars may find therein a certain pleasure, which is why you find them driving here and there for no good reason. Among the various offenses, there is also the fact that the woman becomes free. She goes for what she wants, when she wants and where she wants, because she is alone in her car. She goes out at any hour of the day or night she wants, and may perhaps stay out late. If families nowadays suffer from this when it comes to young men, what would be their reaction to such behavior on the part of young women? Wherever she wishes, right or left, she may travel the length and breadth of the country and even possibly go abroad. Among further offenses this could cause a woman's rebellion against her family, and against her husband. At the slightest annoyance, she leaves her home and goes off in her car, to somewhere she may breathe and find relief. This also occurs with certain young men, although they have a greater capacity to put up with things than women. Among the offenses, again, there is the specter of debauchery: when stopped at road signs, in petrol stations, at checkpoints, or by traffic officers when investigating a crime or an accident; or even when stopped to put air in tires, or indeed in case of a breakdown on the road, the woman driver will need help. So what will become of her then? Perhaps she encounters a perverted

man who makes advances at her, and takes advantage of her honor, in exchange for helping her out of her difficulty. Especially if her need for help reaches a certain degree of urgency. Among the offenses is also the rise of accidents: women, by their nature, are less confident, less objective and have lesser capacities than men. So if the woman is assailed by danger, she will be incapable of acting. Among the offenses is the extra money women drivers will cost their overworked husbands. It is a fact that, by her very nature, a woman is superfluous in anything to do with clothing. Do you not see how attached women are to what they wear? As soon as a new fashion emerges, women make a dash to have it even if it is uglier than what they have already. Do you not see how the walls of her bedroom are decorated? By deduction, this fickleness will be more pronounced for the car, for every time a new model comes out, the woman will abandon the old car for the new!"*

All this, needless to say, is sheer rambling, falsification. There is nothing in the religious writings to support this kind of assertion. This claimed fatwa is based merely on personal statements; it is easy to see the contrast with the method practiced by experts in Muslim law. Religion is not a matter of personal opinion. This is just another example which helps us to see the true face of the Wahhabi ideology.

---

* *Al-Moudjahid*, 43, June 1996.

7

THE BRAINWASHING OF ZACARIAS

In the summer of 1996 my wife and I decided to take a holiday in Morocco. I knew Zacarias would probably come to France, as he did every summer, but I didn't know exactly when. I hadn't heard a whisper out of him for a whole year.

I hadn't been to Morocco in nineteen years. I was eager to see the other members of my family, to see their faces again. The last time was when I was ten. My grandmother, my aunt, my uncles and cousins—what had become of them? It's true that I knew only a fraction of my many relatives, but I was very fond of them, and they of me. There were many I'd only talked to on the phone; seeing them in Morocco would be putting faces to voices. The thought of meeting them all filled me with joy. I got ready for our journey well in advance, like an impatient child waiting for his birthday. I gave my car a tune-up. Then, suddenly, it was time. We stopped to say goodbye to all our friends, and I called the family to tell them we were on our way.

We got off to a good early evening start, but before long the car began acting up. The fan belt was up to its old tricks. Rather than turn around and head back to Montpellier, we decided to take our chances with the engine. So we drove down through Spain with the car in a pitiful state. I didn't stop to sleep, and covered nearly 1,000 miles in one go. When we got to Algeciras, I called the family to let them know we were okay and we boarded the ferry. I was exhausted but in good spirits.

The Mediterranean crossing seemed to last forever, though it took only two hours. Finally, Tangier loomed on the horizon. After nineteen years, I was looking at Morocco once more, land of my forefathers; the contrast of the white houses against the deep blue of the sea was dazzling. We disembarked, and Fouzia's father, my uncle—and now my father-in-law, too—was there to meet us. A moving gesture: he'd driven 200 miles to welcome us.

We had an important appointment as soon as we landed. Sheik Abdel Aziz ibn As-Siddiq Al-Ghummaari, a renowned Sunni theological scholar and author of many books about the Prophetic tradition, religious law, and Sufi teachings, was to receive us at his home. His brother, Sheik Abdallah, who had written widely against Wahhabism, enjoyed an even greater renown. Their father was one of the distinguished *mutjahid* in Islam.* The imam at the At-Tawba Mosque in Montpellier, where I'd been taking theology courses for a couple years, had recommended that I seek counsel from him.

Sheik As-Siddiq received us most warmly in his home in the old medina. He ushered us into his large Moroccan living room, which must have measured a good thirty feet square. Bench seats along the walls and low, carved wood tables conveyed all the beauty of Moroccan craftsmanship. A magnificent chandelier hung in the

---

* *Mutjahid* are juridical scholars with the highest credentials, capable of interpreting the laws of Islam on basic points that may have been the subject of previous *ijmaa*—consensus of *Mutjahid* scholars on a subject to do with Islam in any area. It is not merely the unanimous agreement of any group of Muslims, or even of non-*Mutjahid* scholars, about an issue of Islam. Some of the leading scholars are Ash-Shafii, Malik, Ahmad ibn Hambal, Abu Hanifah, and their peers.

middle of a ceiling of ornate plaster. It was all very attractive. We talked in quiet tones about the instruction I was receiving, and the sheik encouraged me to continue along my path. After about an hour I changed tack: I'd also come to ask him about my brother. Because I was worried. Just before leaving, my sister Jamila had let me in on a secret. The previous year Zacarias had been to see her and had said, "Abd Samad and Fouzia are doing *tawassul,* they're heathens. Be on your guard with them, but whatever else happens, don't say anything to them."

Tawassul is an invocation in which a person asks Allah to grant him a favor, or to help him to avoid a problem, by citing the name of a prophet or saint. For example: "I ask Allah, through the Prophet Muhammad [☝], to grant me piety." The Wahhabis believe that this is akin to idolatry. In their book, "no one may use an intermediary to address Allah." Yet it is the prophet himself who taught a blind man to say: "Oh Allah, I beseech Thee and turn to Thee through our Prophet Muhammad [☝], the Prophet of mercy. Oh Muhammad [☝], I turn through Thee to my Lord so that my need may be filled. Oh Allah, accept his intercession in my favour and my intercession in favour of my own person."

But Wahhabis are extremists; their rejection of the *tawassul* is a pretext for declaring that all Muslims in the world are heathens and idolaters who must be dealt with. When Jamila told me what my brother had said, it made me feel sick—literally. I ended up in the emergency room with shooting pains in my stomach. Zacarias' argument instantly reminded me of Wahhabi beliefs, and I'd never suspected that my bright, well-educated brother, with his stalwart character, could possibly be taken in by that ideology. Plus, he had insisted that Jamila remain silent, a sign that he was wary of me personally.

I, who had seen and understood nothing for all those days spent with him, maybe all those years. Now the oddness of his behavior came flooding back to mind. Now I made new sense of his silences and his sadness, what I took to be depression. Maybe he was ill at ease with Fouzia and me because he regarded us simply as heathens? And to think that he didn't seem to be interested in religion! I spent hours and hours thinking about it, going over the tiniest details of his visits to France. I had trouble believing that the abyss I glimpsed was real.

I had to be clear in my mind about it. So I asked Sheik As-Siddiq for advice. I told him what Jamila had told me. He listened in silence. When I'd finished, the sheik said: "Your brother is a Wahhabi. And the Wahhabis are dangerous. You must be on your guard, beware the Wahhabi creed." For an hour the sheik told me all about Wahhabis. He stressed that they were a violent people. When we left his house, I knew that my brother was in danger—or worse, was himself dangerous.

When finally we joined the whole family, I told them about my conversation with Sheik As-Siddiq. Some of them then told me that earlier that year my brother had made a whirlwind visit to Morocco. His behavior had been more than strange; nobody had understood what was going on. Everything for him was forbidden (*haram*), but he was contradicting himself. So he would forbid others to smoke and yet he would go to a corner of the building and smoke cigarettes. Everywhere Zacarias went in Morocco, I was told, he left a disconcerting impression.

On the bright side, I saw my grandmother again. It was a very touching reunion. She took me by the hand and said: "Come, I will give you a lesson in religion." Then she became somber. "I saw your brother a few months ago. He was behaving strangely and saying untrue things about religion. So I want you to pay attention. Watch out for those who are called *ikhwan muslimin* (Muslim brotherhood), for they more deserve the name *ikhwan moujrimin* (criminal brotherhood). They do abominable things in the name of Islam. No, my son, Islam has never said to do what they are doing."

There were more surprises in store for Fouzia and me. After returning to France a few weeks later, we went to Narbonne to see Jamila. And Zacarias had just been there.

To start with, she was taken aback by his appearance. Zacarias wore a full beard and had a shaven head. He was wearing trousers which came to mid-calf. But above all it was his behavior that shocked her. One morning, she told us, she put on a lengthy, short-sleeved dress to go shopping. Zacarias snapped, "You're not going to go out looking like a whore!" Jamila was shocked and replied, "What do you mean talking to your sister like that? What's the matter with you? What's up?" Zacarias then mumbled a few incomprehensible words and went to his room. A few moments later, he came back out crying, and collapsed on the sofa, asking her to forgive him. Jamila didn't understand a thing, but she saw that he was suffering. He was her kid brother, and she comforted him.

When she told me all that, I realized that my brother was in a bad way. He was going through a most painful internal struggle. Jamila also told me that Zacarias had left her some religious books and urged her to read them. He told her that he would be calling her and giving her advice over the phone. And in fact he did call her a few weeks later—and flew into a rage when she admitted that she hadn't read the books. My sister gave me the books. Needless to say, they were Wahhabi texts.

But that wasn't all. Zacarias had raised a stir in the Narbonne mosque. He went to the Friday sermon, when the mosque was full of young people. My brother addressed them: "I'm going to give you a lesson." The congregation was surprised but polite, and let him speak. And Zacarias started to explain the Wahhabi creed. The young folk, who had a religious education, rejected his nonsense, and the discussion became heated. Just when Zacarias was reciting alleged verses of the Koran in French, the imam walked in. He listened to my brother for a few seconds, and then asked him, "Can you speak Arabic?" Zacarias answered, "No." "So how do you know that what you are saying is the true meaning of what is said in the Koran? You haven't been able to check it in the Book, because it is revealed in Arabic. The Koran reads: 'Nothing resembles Him, and He is the One who hears and sees,' in verse 11 of Surat *ash-Shura*. An extraordinary saint, Dhu l-Nun al-Misri, said, 'Whatever you imagine in your mind, Allah is different therefrom.'"

Zacarias lost his temper. He got to his feet and tried to hit the imam. The young people intervened and threw him out. He walked off hurling insults at them, and calling them *kuffar*—heathens.

From that moment on there were no two ways about it. My brother had been recruited by a sectarian group. But what is a sectarian group? The definition in Webster's International Dictionary, for example, is simple: a "sectarian" person is "one characterized by a narrow and bigoted adherence to a sect." The reality is more complicated. The Wahhabi sect to which Zacarias belonged, if connected to al-Qaeda, is part of a huge creature. Contrary to what the West has long thought, al-Qaeda is highly organized. At the very top is its head, but there are countless tentacles, each one capable of moving independently. The leaders have put a lot of thought into attracting young operatives. They recruit actively in the UK, France, Germany, and elsewhere in Europe; in the UK, where Zacarias was recruited, the process was openly conducted at mosques and in the street. In France they have to be a little more discreet, though this is not necessarily reassuring.

First, they pick out young people who, one way or another, have been estranged from their families. These young people, with no adult to guide them, are cut off from strong moral anchors. The chaotic personal and family history of Zacarias fits the pattern perfectly. I was his only safeguard. But in London, he was far away from me. In the early stages of what can only be called an exile, we talked often on the phone, and he returned regularly to France. On those visits he spoke about his daily life. Then he changed. He had always been quiet, but now he became secretive. He no longer told me about his friends, or how he spent his days, and even less about how he made a living. He also changed physically, his features growing hardened.

I misinterpreted all these changes. First and foremost, I put them down to problems he might be having living abroad. I didn't want to dramatize the situation, so I stuck strictly to my role as elder brother, accommodating, warm, and patient. And I got it all wrong: Zacarias was in the process of ripping up his last roots. The preferred strategy of Wahhabi and Qutbist gurus is to try to cut people off from their families. When the family lives far away, it's easier. I am firmly convinced that someone, even several people, had the precise task of distancing my brother from his family and that brainwashing was involved.

Earlier, I had committed a basic error by sending Zacarias pamphlets warning against Wahhabism. His new acquaintances must have been quick to see the critical spirit that I could induce in their recruit. Zacarias did not just wake up one day and decide that I was a "heathen." The thoughts he expressed to our sister were the culmination of a long process of embitterment. He had doubtless told his manipulators about his family, and they had realized that it wasn't his sister or his mother who represented any real obstacle. There was an urgent need, however, to separate him from me, a Sunni.

Part of the Wahhabi technique involves avoiding all exchanges with Sunnis, demonizing them. Wahhabis accept not the slightest challenge to what they have to say. The fact that the group had successfully gathered information about me from London is further proof, if any were needed, of the range and efficiency of their networks.

Cultural uprooting left my brother particularly vulnerable to the influence of the recruiters. Like most of the young Muslims who headed for London, he knew nothing about the codes of British society, which is not altogether welcoming. Foreigners like Zacarias are tolerated at best, as long as they don't stray too far from their own community.

Zacarias is a French man who is not at ease with being French, and a Moroccan who can't speak Arabic. What community can he call his own? Eventually, his malaise guided him to company he could keep—that of outcasts and extremists.

His indoctrination was greatly hastened by his total ignorance of religion. This was virgin territory. He had no previous training, and no moral weapons with which to defend himself. He would have been much more resistant to brainwashing, I believe, had he grown up in a Sunni tradition, and benefitted from a strong religious culture and foreknowledge of extremist movements.

How did my brother have his first contact with those responsible for his transformation? In London, nothing could be easier. Even today, every Friday outside certain London mosques you can find fanatics extolling the 9-11 attacks. Other mosques are known for the extremist sermons of their imam. The British call this "freedom of speech."

And then, like all sects, these organizations seem wonderfully generous. They run charities with grants from abroad. Zacarias, who sometimes went hungry, told me that when he was hanging out with Algerian immigrants, they were offered meals at the mosques. What easier way to attract someone who is hungry than with a wholesome plateful of food?

The sermons of extremist imams are effective with young people in dire straits because the words reinforce a sense of tragedy. They are filled with the suffering of Muslim people. The listener feels like a victim, all the more because of constant references to the massacres of Chechens, Palestinians, and Algerians (which, needless to say, were not in the early stages the work of the Armed Islamic Group). For Zacarias, these sermons hit home.

The imams use a mixed-message technique to exacerbate identity problems and to cultivate a desire to be militant and struggle against injustice. There is, for example, no distinction made between the suffering of the Palestinian people and that of the Algerian people. Yet the pain of the Algerian having his throat cut by his neighbor has nothing to do with the pain of the Palestinian buried alive beneath his house by an Israeli tank. Add to this a regular reminder of the feelings of exclusion so common among the recruits, and the sense of universal pain overwhelms. And when you suffer you reflect less. It is hard to take a step back to analyze the situation in the cold light of day.

Extremists know how to cultivate people's weaknesses, the better to manipulate them. One such weakness is pride. It is a sweet song to the prideful ear to be promised membership in the religious and intellectual elite, to be above mere mortals. Language, here, is a valuable tool for extremists. Wahhabis have a vocabulary all their own, designed to forge a sense of group cohesion. All those who are not like them are *kuffar*, heathens. Their leaders are *khalifs*, emirs. Warriors are *mujahideen*. These terms do indeed exist in Muslim law, but the Wahhabis give them their own spin.

After several months in these circles, the young recruit is ready. He is presented with a duty, a "mysterious action" he is to execute, supposedly an honor. He "becomes eligible" to go abroad. He may be invited to "go for training" in a camp. Or else to go abroad in order to contact Muslims from other countries, such as Pakistan. Once in the camp, it is easy to make him lose his bearings. He is put through athletic training, and training in weapon handling. These are intensive exercises. He faces increasingly difficult challenges; he is not well fed and is gradually exhausted. After several weeks or months, he gets the feeling that he's not capable of doing what is expected of him. He is embarrassed; he feels guilty because he is incompetent. And yet he is told over and over that others before him have succeeded and gone on to "great things."

At this stage, there are two possible scenarios. The recruit might quit, disillusioned, and make his way back to his old life, perhaps to his home country. I have collected accounts of former recruits such as these.

Or, he carries on. And if he carries on, it is to the bitter end. Because he feels incompetent, the only thing he can do to help the cause is to give his life to it. This will prove to others that, in the end, he was up to their expectations.

He is now ripe for suicide. Wahhabi and Qutbist leaders announce everywhere, including on al-Jazeera, a television station with a large Arab audience, that suicide committed during an attack or an assassination is not a suicide. But the Koran reads: "Do not kill yourself, Allah is merciful to you" (Surat an-Nisaa', verse 29). In addition, Prophet Muhammad [ﷺ] said, "He who kills himself with some thing shall be chastised with that same thing in hell"—a hadith recounted by Al-Bukhari. Thus it is quite clear that Islam forbids suicide. The Koran also reads, "Oh you who believe, be upright for Allah's sake, bearers of witness with justice; and let not hatred of a people incite you not to act equitably. Be just; that is nearer to observance of duty. And keep your duty to Allah. Surely Allah is aware of what you do" (Surah 5 al-Maidah , verse 8).

What could I do to help Zacarias? I felt helpless. He had broken off contact with me. I didn't know his friends and acquaintances in England. My only hope was that he would outgrow this phase. Was he even still in London? Nobody knew.

I don't know exactly how Zacarias succumbed to the Wahhabis. Even today, despite everything I've read and heard, it's a great mystery. How could someone so open, so communicative and warm, how could someone so ambitious, so involved in his studies, so keen to better himself, how could someone like him let himself be swallowed up by such scum?

Sometimes, when I wake up in the morning, I am still overcome to think about him. It still seems unreal. I say to myself, "How is it possible?" Yes, my brother does have his weaknesses, but he also has great inner strength. He proved as much, first by surviving the difficulties of his childhood, and then by throwing himself into his studies. These thoughts are cause for pessimism. I am convinced of one thing: if it worked with my brother, it can work with plenty of other young people.

Perhaps, seeing Zacarias change and become so introspective and silent, I should have been more alarmed. I could have suspected drugs, or a sect, but I didn't. I focused on trying to patch up the shortcomings in our family, on providing him with a stable and affectionate environment. I didn't ask myself the right questions. By the time my sister talked to me, and the pieces of the jigsaw suddenly came together—gestures, startling words, silences—it was too late.

Am I in a position to give advice to families who may be affected by this type of indoctrination? To North African families I can only say: make sure that your children have the foundations of religious culture. Knowledge is the only possible weapon in the face of the ideologies of terror. Society has great influence, but it cannot crack a strong family circle. Other people had childhoods that were even worse than mine and my siblings'—of this I am well aware. But none of us has emerged unscathed. Today, my sisters Nadia and Jamila are traumatized. My brother Zacarias stands accused of a horrendous crime, and is rotting in an American prison. If there is any point in giving advice, I would ask society to learn to fight against racial discrimination and social exclusion.

What is surprising is that those who have a voice, through the media, do not address the roots of the problem. Though they condemn attacks and assassinations, they do not denounce Wahhabi ideologists (Abd al-Wahhab, Ibn Baz, and Al-Uthaymeen) and Muslim Brotherhood ideologists (Qutb, Al-Mawdudi, and Al-Qaradawi). People of goodwill must be united in denouncing and ostracizing those who espouse the destructive ideology of these terrorist movements. Politicians must make sure that we do not ourselves become the executioners' accomplices, be it out of ignorance or mere laxity.

8

ZACARIAS IS NOT A ONE-OFF CASE

At this juncture, I would like to describe briefly what happened to Xavier, one of my classmates.

I met Xavier in Perpignan. I'd just moved to the second year of advanced vocational training and he was starting his first year. I was 23, he about 20. He'd come from Montpellier. He was a strapping young man, an impressive six-foot-one, and well-built. Girls found his smile seductive. He was as kind as he was physically striking. Above all, Xavier had a very subtle wit and a contagious cheerfulness. I quite literally would laugh until I cried when I was with him. When he came to the evening meals we would make at our place, you were sure of having a good time. Xavier had a way of telling stories that made us laugh so hard we couldn't catch our breaths. For him, nothing was ever dramatic. He was refined, lively, and fun. I had been living in Perpignan long enough to have a pretty full address book. There were boys and girls in it; the list of girls particularly interested Xavier. He was so likeable that we very quickly became inseparable.

That guy had something difficult to define, perhaps it was just charm. He had a way of being that meant that you forgave him many things. Even when he exaggerated, he did it with such ingenuousness that everybody cracked up. One day, he drove Fouzia and Zacarias and me to Montpellier. While we were looking for a parking space, a driver just ahead of us with a big car found a slot, leisurely pulled up beside the car ahead, switched on his right indicator, started to reverse—and stopped dead. Xavier had already parked our car in the spot and we were getting out. The guy hadn't even noticed. Dumbfounded, he rolled down his window to bawl us out, but Xavier was one step ahead of him and, with a beaming smile, said, "So sorry, I didn't see you!" Never mind that the guy was driving a monster four-wheel drive. Voices were raised, but Xavier laughed in such a delightful way that the man started laughing too. That's Xavier for you.

But there was something else, something more profound that bound us together. We both knew how painful life could be. Xavier had one particular thing in common with Zac and me. Because he was black, he *knew*, in his bones, what racism meant. We shared practically the same skin color. There was no need to discuss it. We both knew perfectly well what the other could experience and feel in that respect. Xavier, who was from Africa, had kept the habit of calling whites *toubabs*. Sometimes, with a bitter irony, he would say: "*Toubabs* really like their house nigger, the one who makes them laugh…"

Xavier, other friends, and I spent the year partying. At the end of the academic year, I left Perpignan, but I didn't leave Xavier. For me he was a real friend. I was very fond of him. He was incredibly generous.

A year later, when Xavier finished his advanced vocational diploma, Zacarias had been in Great Britain for several months. He came back to France regularly, and because Xavier and I were still seeing a lot of each other, my brother and he often crossed paths. Zacarias told Xavier, as well as other friends, how he'd managed to get onto an interesting university course, just the way he had wanted. And he told them how, at the end of that course, he would obtain a Master of International Business (MIB). For his friends from class, that was like an advanced business school with a little bit extra—a degree obtained in England looks good on your resumé. And some of the friends felt tempted. Zacarias told Xavier he could help him get started. He now knew London well, all the crucial ins and outs. He also knew how to prepare for the entrance exam for the MIB, because he had successfully done it. Anyway, Zac was a reliable guy, a friend you could count on.

Xavier thought about those new prospects and made up his mind. In 1993, he and a classmate went to see Zacarias in London. The classmate, Hartium, told me nothing special happened to begin with. Xavier passed his entrance exam for the MIB and attended his classes. So it had worked out for him. He would come back to France more or less when Zacarias did. He came to see his family, especially his mother, to whom he was very attached. He would also see us and other friends. He also told us that British society was to say the least double-edged; on the surface very tolerant, because you came across every nationality over there. But in reality, he said, each community lived in its own ghetto. The segregation between blacks and whites seemed to him much more marked than in France. When he came back, he was fun and funny as ever, and much appreciated by everybody. He spent most of his time with Zacarias. One summer, they went on holiday together to Senegal.

In January, 1995, I saw Xavier for the last time. We spent several evenings together with my wife. I still have photos of one evening. One of them shows him sitting on our bed, in our little apartment. In the photo, he has very short hair and he is smiling broadly at the camera. He has a cigarette in his right hand. In another photo he is sprawled across the bed, roaring with laughter, head down, eyes all creased, laughing so hard. Xavier had just told us that he had converted to Islam and chosen Yusuf as his Muslim first name. But he didn't seem to be a practising Muslim, and he didn't pray. His behavior was just the same. He talked to me about the Regent's Park mosque, telling me proudly that he had shared a couscous there with Yusuf Islam, the ex-singer formerly known as Cat Stevens. Then he returned to England to continue his studies and I never saw him again.

Zacarias, for his part, came to France in the early summer. He announced to me that he had received his MIB. When he went back to London, it was to pick up his degree. I went with him to the airport. I was proud of him because, despite all the problems, he had achieved his goal. I didn't know at the time that it was the last time I would see my brother, until after September 11, in the media…

It was during the summer of 1996, on our return from Morocco, that I noticed a marked change in Xavier. I had just realized that my brother had been recruited by Wahhabis, when I discovered to my amazement that Xavier, too, had adopted their arguments. What my Montpellier friends then told me left me dumbfounded. Xavier had arrived, introduced himself as my friend, and tried to get his message across. This occurred at the very same time, and with the very same arguments, as Zacarias in the Narbonne mosque. The coincidence was more than disturbing. I drew the conclusion that the Wahhabis had succeeded in indoctrinating a new convert. I was sincerely upset for him. Xavier's brother, whom I met in Montpellier on several occasions, told me that he also was very worried. He didn't understand what was happening. He told me that Xavier had told them he had gone to Kuwait with Zacarias, apparently to learn religion. "Learn religion! Learn Wahhabism, more like!" I replied. And I explained the movement to him. I knew that in Kuwait there were major establishments teaching Wahhabism.

Xavier's brother told me that they had all seen Xavier gradually changing as well. But because they didn't know anything about Islam, they thought for a long time that all Muslims behaved like that. When they realized that his behavior was abnormal and the change in him far too abrupt, it was once again too late.

I offered that brother, who was as devastated as I was, the only advice that seemed to me to be realistic: not to burn his bridges with Xavier. He and I felt so helpless in front of such changes. We just didn't understand how these two guys, both of them lovers of life, could have let themselves be indoctrinated like that. We parted telling each other that perhaps it was all just the craziness of youth, and it would pass.

I did not understand how my younger brother had concluded that it was acceptable to strike us out of his life. It hurt me. I had always thought that our shared years of suffering had woven indestructible bonds. It was as if a part of me had been amputated. I had to suffer in silence. There is one thing that worsens my distress: throughout all those years of absence, nobody bothered to find out what had become of Zacarias. I had the feeling that I was the only person who remembered him.

What really is this Wahhabism which breaks up families? I have read in textbooks and history books about the bloody and destructive consequences of Wahhabism, and the ideology of the Muslim Brotherhood. But for me those are just words. In my gut and in my heart, through these pangs of anguish which awake me at night, I understand that the reality behind the ideology is suffering and injustice. Now whenever I meet a young—or a not-so-young—person who engages me in a sectarian argument, I try to guide that person back to more moderate thinking, backed up by proof. If necessary, I share my experience with him. I describe how extremism has taken my brother away. I think I have understood that it is important not to give a free rein to Wahhabis and the Muslim Brotherhood. So I'm involved in preventive work. Now I can clearly see the relevance of the warnings of the imam at the At-Tawba mosque. In 1992, I started to go to the Association of Islamic Welfare Projects (APBIF) in France, whose members were the only people to have warned me against the danger of the Wahhabis.

One day, in the year 2000, I was summoned by the Montpellier police. A policeman ushered me into an office and asked me to sit down. With no further ado, and in complete silence, they showed me a color photocopy of a page from a website. On the page there was an article about the war in Chechnya with three color photos, all of Xavier. In the first photo, taken outdoors, he was standing behind two other soldiers, wearing a military uniform and a dark cap pulled down around his ears. He was smiling at the camera with the forefinger of his right hand raised. The second photo showed him in profile, again in a military uniform. He had a thin moustache and a long beard. His head was shaved. He wasn't smiling any more, but holding his chin in his hand, apparently deep in thought. In the last photo, he was lying alongside other men, with a blanket pulled up over him. His right leg was covered in blood. His eyes were closed. He looked as if he was asleep, not in pain. The photo had a caption; the words leapt out at me, searing my eyes: "Massoud Al-Benin, born in France, lived in London, died in Chechnya."

Xavier. The article accompanying the photo announced his death on April 12, 2000. I read it, understanding nothing, full of disbelief. I felt like crying. Tears welled up, but I managed not to break down in front of the policemen, who hadn't exactly handled me with kid gloves. They asked me if I knew where my brother was. "The French government," they told me, "would like to warn French nationals about the risks they are taking." So they obviously thought that my brother was with Xavier, unless he was still in

Chechnya, or going there soon. I didn't know what to think any more. I expected the worst, but deep down hoped for the best.

Every day after that I found myself expecting to hear that my brother was dead. You never get used to such an idea. I told myself that possibly he had already died in some far-flung corner of the world, and that I would never know about it. Now I have a better understanding of the determination of families of people who have disappeared to want to know the truth about the fate of their nearest and dearest. I lived with this expectation until the tragedy of September 11.

9

THE MEDIA STORM

On September 11, 2001, I was in class with my students. On television we watched the second airplane crash and explode in one of the World Trade Center towers. We were stunned by those terrifying images. There was an instant flood of questions: Who? Why? How was it be possible? In the United States! At that moment we imagined perhaps tens of thousands of deaths. All those people who had set off that morning saying "See you tonight" to their families. They would never see them again. The two towers collapsed one after the other, and the vision of horror worsened. I knew that there were people of all nationalities and all religions in the Twin Towers. Once again, the victims were civilians.

Driving back to Montpellier, I learned that a certain "Franco-Algerian Zacarias Moussaoui" might be involved. The impact of those images had me feeling immediately concerned. I instantly felt close to all that pain. But when I heard that announcement, I felt dizzy. I had the impression of teetering into the void, into somewhere unknown, that I felt to be tragic. I had a hunch that I was about to be crushed. I was summoned by the police on September 14, and they told me about Zacarias' situation. He had been in prison since August 16, and was an FBI suspect. When I left the police station I felt completely shattered. For the past few years I'd been expecting the worst, but hanging on to a sliver of hope. I thought about my mother and sisters. How were they living through this disaster? Fouzia and I thought about going to see them. We thought that our pain might perhaps bring us all together again. Then I had to get back to work.

The first articles about Zacarias Moussaoui started to appear. That was the beginning of the slander and libel about my wife and me. They said that I was a member of the Muslim Brotherhood. They said my brother and I were terrorists, me a sleeper, him active. My wife was also allegedly a former Muslim Brotherhood member, and responsible for Zacarias' downward spiral. Some articles reported unattributed, insulting comments about Fouzia: "Cancer had entered our house," and "I didn't know that I'd let the wolf into the fold." As if it were necessary to add insult to all this injury, certain papers said that my mother was the author of these remarks. Fouzia and I were shocked and alarmed. We just couldn't believe it. I didn't understand anything any more. I couldn't imagine that my mother would take advantage of the situation to settle a score. I was tired of the family rows and had kept my distance, hoping that time would heal those wounds and enable us to come together again one day.

But no such luck. Just violence, lies, libel and people stooping to anything. That's what I was finding in the papers and that's what was being attributed to my mother. I'd never talked about those family rows. Anyone can understand that it's not nice to hear bad things said about yourself, and in the case of Fouzia and myself, it was the entire international press that was echoing these libellous accusations. Those lies were serious because they had to do with a real tragedy, and several thousand deaths. Certain people had no respect for our dignity as human beings. At school, a colleague thrust an article before my eyes in which it was written that I was close to the Muslim Brotherhood movement. And he said to me, "I want some explanations." People would look away when I walked by, and there was silence when I walked into the teacher's lounge. Some colleagues suddenly seemed very busy, and gradually the room would empty out. Everybody said they had things to do. I was totally distraught, because I felt that the press campaign might have catastrophic consequences for my job. I'd been working in the state education system for twelve years, the last six teaching electrical engineering as an assistant. This means that I do not have tenure, and at every new school year am assigned to a different school. It would be easy not to give me any post at all.

When the events of September 11 shook the face of the earth, I had been working for two weeks at the vocational school in Mende. So my new colleagues had hardly had time to get to know me. Then all of a sudden they were seeing my name in the press. From one day to the next, they found themselves working side by side with the brother of a presumed terrorist linked to massive carnage. Many of my colleagues avoided the subject. When I was present they talked about hunting and cooking. The whole world was asking questions about that tragedy, but they went to great pains not to broach the issue in my presence. Maybe some of them weren't sure how to talk about it with me. Maybe they were afraid of going too far in their conclusions, or maybe they believed the lies about me, and saw me as a latent terrorist. I summoned my courage and decided to deal with the situation. I would talk to all those of good will. I certainly would not isolate myself. I would take the initiative, bring my colleagues together, and explain candidly to them what was going on.

I did it during a 10:00 coffee break in the common room. The whole faculty was there. Against stony silence, I told them what I thought about it all. I told them that I was a Muslim, and that I in no way espoused the ideology of terror and destruction. I explained to them that all those newspapers had been lying and that I had never had any connections with any terrorists. A colleague spoke out loud enough so that everybody could hear, "Don't worry. As far as I'm concerned, I believe you, not the papers." Many of them told me how deeply my situation was affecting them. The most recurrent questions were, Where were the ethics and morality in all this? Where was the human aspect? In the days that followed, lots of newspapers, and radio and television reports continued to bombard the public with information, true or false. My colleagues didn't know what to think. I got the impression that they too felt overtaken by events.

I soon went back to Montpellier. It was a two-and-a-half hour drive, so I had plenty of time to think. I was quite sure that I should reply to all those lies. But how? With whom? Who would agree to hear me out? I didn't know how, but I knew I had to do something. I reached Montpellier at ten in the evening. A friend who was devastated by what he'd been reading in the newspapers had kept press clippings for me. Journalists were waiting for me from Canal+, France 2, TF1. They wanted an interview. I felt tremendous pressure, heightened by everything I read in those clippings. I was tired after my drive, but now I felt angry. My disappointment ran deep. I still couldn't believe that my mother had gone so far as to unjustly accuse my wife and myself of such serious things, in such a terrifying context. Yes, spiritual instruction does teach us that it's better to be the victim than the oppressor. But being the victim of injustice leaves a bitter taste in the mouth. Fouzia and I jointly decided to state our case. We decided not to answer the libellous accusations, neither in the media nor in the courts. In this tragic situation, we thought it was far more useful to warn against generalizations that lump Muslims and terrorists together.

I sought to protect what was left of my privacy: my home. So I asked the imam if I could use the mosque to conduct interviews with the journalists. He agreed. As it so happened, on September 9 the mosque had hosted a forum of associations. Several hundred associations had presented their activities and their goals. The forum lasted all day and filled a whole neighborhood of Montpellier. So I had access to leftover presentations laying out Muslim beliefs, introducing the principles of Islam, retracing the historical and geographical spread of Muslims throughout the world and showing the range of architecture that exists in the Muslim world. The point was to show that Islam builds and does not destroy, with striking parallels between Roman architecture and Arabic-Muslim architecture throughout the world. What came across was that Westerners have accepted and incorporated Islam in their own architectural tradition. There also were presentations explaining why the principles of Islam are opposed to the Wahhabi and Qutbist ideologies.

Until two in the morning, I explained my brother's story to a succession of journalists. I showed them the information tables and the pamphlets warning against terrorism and extremism, which had been published in the mosque for years. I told them that I hadn't seen my brother since 1995, that I hadn't been passive and inactive. On the contrary, I had made my contribution to various social and cultural causes. I tried to get them to understand, to point out to them that the task of warning against extremism is a day-to-day task, precise and methodical, vital. This was why my wife and I felt cheated and scorned, as if people wanted to deny our opinions by labelling us as extremists and fanatics. With the newspapers dragging our names through the mud, my social involvement and my work with clubs was being dismissed.

Some of the people who came to meet me didn't just want to know about the life of the alleged terrorist Zacarias Moussaoui. They were also keen to meet the brother who was supposed to share the same ideas, and see his wife, who was probably the brains behind the whole thing. Needless to say, this did not make for easy first contacts with the press. Several journalists told me later that they had arrived suspicious, wary, sometimes even worried. One woman had been paralyzed with fear. After talking with us for twenty minutes, she phoned her husband to tell him that she was all right and that we were normal people, so there was no need for him to worry. What exactly were they expecting?

I realized that the mosque was totally misunderstood as a place of worship. Most of those journalists had never set foot inside a mosque, and they were visibly ill-at-ease there. There was a lot of confusion. Some thought they didn't have the right to go inside. That bothered me, because I realized that plenty of journalists knew nothing at all about their country's second-largest religion. I even wondered if some of them weren't being ignorant on purpose, such was their glaring lack of culture. Some find something "shady" about a Muslim praying five times a day; he must be a fundamentalist or on the way to becoming one. He is seen as fatalistic and rigid, with a cumbersome, not to say eccentric, religious practice. For some, it was a bit as if all Muslims were potential extremists, at least until proven to the contrary.

My close friends and my family were all deeply shocked by what they were reading in the press. I wouldn't wish this kind of traumatizing experience on anyone. For me, a professional journalist is someone who gets out there, investigates, double-checks his information and confirms it through various sources. He's certainly not someone who's content with just one side of a story. Luckily, my wife, friends, and the imam of the mosque were there that night to back me up.

Three weeks had gone by since September 11. The media storm turned into a hurricane: *Le Monde, Le Parisien, Le Figaro,*

Libération, France Soir, Le Progrès de Lyon, L'Indépendent de Perpignan, Le Midi Libre, L'Express, Le Point, VSD, Paris Match, Courrier International, Le Nouvel Observateur, La Gazette de Montpellier, Le Journal du Dimanche, Al-Hayat (an Arab newspaper published in London), *NRC Handelsblad* (a Dutch newspaper), *Le Maroc International Hebdo, The Times, The Sunday Times,* TFI, France 2, France 3, La Cinquième, M6, LCI, CBS News, MTV Info and AM (German TV stations), NetWORK (a Dutch channel), ABC, Channel 4, CNN, NHK (a Japanese channel), an Australian public service channel, France Info, Radio France International, RMC, the Dow Jones agency...

The TV crews usually consisted of a journalist, a sound tech and a cameraman. Press crews had a journalist and a photographer. Sometimes the same channel sent several crews. In the mad rush of it all, Fouzia and I split various tasks. Fouzia dealt with looking over what was in the press, rights of reply and any followup there might be (no media published any denials), and also organized my appointments. The imam at the mosque received journalists, answered their questions, and spent hours explaining to them how, from a religious standpoint, the terror ideology had no foundations. In the mosque, journalists were given tea and cakes, and the people at the reception desks tirelessly answered the ever-ringing phone. They kept the journalists company and made them wait their turn. Everybody was hospitable.

Yet some journalists left quite a lot to be desired when it came to being tactful, and certainly didn't beat around the bush. One journalist asked me, "Is it true that you're a fundamentalist?" Was he hoping I'd say "Yes"? Some, displeased that I hadn't granted them an interview, would go into a huddle with their colleagues and portray me as an extremist. Others used hidden cameras, even though the mosque was open to them and nobody was hiding anything. On the other hand, some tried to learn and understand things, taking a close look both at the task of warning against extremism, and at the education and instruction going on in the mosque. I came across some journalists who did their job with professionalism and humanity. There was nothing smug about the way they went about their work. Others, with fewer scruples, wrote articles as if they had met me, when they hadn't even left their desks or taken the trouble to phone me. When I expressed outrage at that practice, they told me it was par for the course. Journalists often work from articles that have already been published, and these are the sole "sources" they use to write their piece. They also explained to me that for them it wasn't surprising to find the same lies cropping up in different newspapers, because local correspondents often freelance for several papers at the same time. They call this the "snowball" effect. In my case, the correspondent of a local paper went to interview my mother and took down what she had to say in exchange for cash. He published an article that was taken up by another local correspondent who worked for several local and national newspapers. This information was then taken up with international press agencies. And that's how I got to be labelled an extremist, a fanatic, and a dormant terrorist. People even made Fouzia responsible for Zacarias being brainwashed and recruited: "It all just has to be a woman's fault!" Fouzia's image in the papers was a caricature, verging on racism. It was the image of an intellectually limited woman, who advocated that men shouldn't do the washing up. In another context, we might have laughed it off, we found it so ridiculous. Psychologically, it was very hard. Fouzia and I felt totally denied as human beings. The thoughts people attributed to us were the very opposite of our values, our convictions and our moral codes. We were the victims of stereotyping whereby everyone conspired to make "Muslim" synonymous with "terrorist."

My wife and I were not the only ones to have been traumatized. In the great media stampede, the congregation at the mosque wavered between indignation—sections of the press denigrated their religion—and fear. They were in fact afraid of reprisals against the mosque. In the United States, a Sikh had been murdered because he'd been taken for a Muslim, because of his beard and the turban on his head. Insulting letters and even death threats were sent to the mosque. One day a giant of a man turned up there asking to see me. I wasn't around, so he left a message: "Tell Abd Samad that he had better watch out what he says or he might have problems." And he drove off in his red four-wheel drive with British plates. Apparently I was getting on certain people's nerves. Not only was my reputation being smeared, but the libel was endangering my wife, me, mosques, and Muslims in general.

We eventually realized that certain journalists weren't interested in what we had to say; our arguments disturbed them. It would all be so much more thrilling if we really were extremists—and above all, the story would sell better. These journalists saw a kind of crime novel and made monsters of the characters involved. Despite all these upheavals, I tried to stay cool, calm and collected, day after day. It didn't stop for three months. Then the breaker would became a wavelet, but before long it would start all over again—every time anyone talked about my brother, or his silence, or the legal proceedings now under way.

Some time later, a journalist from a weekly asked me to help him to write an article. I spent hours working with him. He never asked if he could get in touch with Fouzia. When the article appeared, all I found in it was malicious gossip and lies about my wife. Once again, what was said about her was attributed to my mother. Fouzia observed, "This type of attitude raises three questions: if it's acceptable to write this kind of article because I'm a Muslim, then it shows intolerance; if it's because I'm Moroccan, then it shows racism; and if it's because I'm a woman, then it shows sexism and misogyny." For me, that guy was a stupid idiot who used the pain and blindness of one woman to hurt another.

10

BY WAY OF CONCLUSION

The sacred religious writings in the Holy Koran teach justice and moderation. The wisdom of nations must be learned mutually among peoples. Thus, we read in the Koran the Word of Allah: "O mankind, surely We have created you from a male and a female, and made you tribes and families that you may know each other. Surely the noblest of you with Allah is the most dutiful of you" (Sura 49, verse 13, *Al-Hujurat*). And further: "Let not hatred of a people— because they hindered you from the Sacred Mosque—incite you to transgress. And help one another in righteousness and piety and help not one another in sin and aggression" (Sura 5, verse 2, *Al-Maidah*). God orders us to be a community of justice, fairness and the happy medium. God says this in the Holy Koran: "And thus We have made you an exalted nation that you may be the bearers of witness to the people and [that] the messenger may be a bearer of witness to you" (Sura 2, verse 143, *Al-Baqarah*).

The Koran also teaches us to be concerned with the best works, goodness, charity and fairness to obtain the elevation of the soul: "And every one has a goal to which he turns, so vie with one another in good works"(Sura 2, verse 148, *Al-Baqarah*). The Koran teaches us to discuss in a tolerant manner: "Call to the way of thy Lord with wisdom and goodly exhortation, and argue with them in the best manner" (Sura 16, verse 125, *An-Nahl*). It teaches us to prefer indulgence while giving the right to apply justice: "And if you take your turn, then punish with the like of that with which you were afflicted. But if you show patience, it is certainly best for the patient" (Sura 16, verse 126, *An-Nahl*). These are the true precepts of a Muslim religious education.

What is the current situation with young Muslim people in France? Looking back over my life to date, and my brother's, I can identify with those hundreds of thousands of young people. The lack of parental authority, a difficult childhood, poor education without any goals and without religious references, awash in ignorance about the cultural heritage of their countries of origin, and exclusion everywhere you look. Nowadays I wonder if I'm not a survivor. Could I too have been ensnared, the way my brother was, by extremist groups? Thank the lord that the people who introduced me to Islam taught me that attachment to religion means an adherence to moderation. Prophet Muhammad [ﷺ] said: "Guard against exaggeration in matters of religion."[*]

The more the young Muslim turns his back on religion, the more vulnerable he is. Nowadays the danger of false religious people, dealing in exclusion and extremism, lies in wait for us everywhere. The only bulwarks I know reside in traditional religious culture, in parental support and presence, and in a real policy of struggle against all forms of exclusion, demagogy, and political cant.

---

[*] *Hadith* reported in the *Sunnan* of Ibn Majah.

EPILOGUE

WHO PAYS THE PRICE?

The victims of attacks are of all nationalities, all origins, all skin colors and all religions, be it in Egypt, Algeria, or New York. Then there are the families of victims who survive the death of their loved one, and there are the friends of those who have disappeared who are also traumatized by this barbarity.

There are Muslims the world over who are under suspicion, and being wrongly accused. Muslims are the victims of the sweeping generalization: "Islam equals terrorism." There is Islam, which people attempt to discredit and which is nevertheless innocent of all this fanaticism and all this terror. There are also the families of all those implicated and suspected of being involved in the attacks. Families who are confused, lamenting their pain and incomprehension in the face of tragedy. They would like to think that it is a nightmare and yet all this is very real. Every day, all these victims experience suffering and sadness.

There is one last major victim: the just causes of all oppressed and crushed Muslim peoples. Those Afghans, Chechens and Bosnians who see themselves championed by international Wahhabism. To survive, they stumble from wars of liberation and resistance into extremist traps. Wahhabi fanatics, supported by brainwashed young people through a Qutbist doctrine of massive excommunication, monopolize and engulf just causes. They infiltrate them with financial wealth and weaponry worthy of powerful states. Wahhabis make the most of war to infiltrate local populations, in particular the youth they are so keen to indoctrinate. From this nursery, they will pluck the most fanatical and use them as weapons of destruction everywhere in the world. And when they start to attack civilians and provoke the enemy, they shake up all the dignitaries in those populations and relegate them to the background. Wahhabis whittle away what prestige they do have and force them out. This hostage-taking has political and financial ends, with foreign powers as the beneficiaries. To achieve this goal, Wahhabis first attack religious traditions, doing away with them and then suppressing the rampart of moderate and tolerant religious principles around which Muslim populations rally. Then they physically attack the religious and political authority in these populations. They even go so far to incite terror as to make despicable attacks against civilians on both sides. The earliest defenders of just causes are now stripped of their arguments. They become the victims of those who have taken their causes hostage.

In France, the various sources of information estimate the number of young people enrolled annually in bin Laden's training camps at between 80 and 300. This means that between 80 and 300 families are affected. So these are not isolated cases, but rather a blight on society. French, Americans, Franco-Moroccans, Franco-Algerians, Australians, Belgians, Yemenis, Lebanese, Egyptians. They come from many different countries, so we are facing a problem of international scope.

If we are sincerely interested in bringing this spiral of terror to an end, we cannot skim over a certain number of unsettling questions. Why do some countries make it easy for Wahhabis and parties like the Muslim Brotherhood to spread their propaganda? The careers of all those young people allegedly implicated in the attacks passed by way of Great Britain. Why have the British authorities been so lax? It is well known to one and all that American secret services supported bin Laden for twenty years. How could they be unaware of the dangers represented by that? Why, in France, do the authorities still deal with organizations and individuals who lay claim to ideologies based on terror?

Do we also need our own September 11 to finally open our eyes?

ABOUT THE AUTHORS

ABD SAMAD MOUSSAOUI is a teacher in a technical high school in Narbonne, France.

FLORENCE BOUQUILLAT is a TV journalist at France 2.